THE STORY OF
TRUMP

While you can never be sure just what you're going to get when it comes to the Don, there's one thing you can always bank on: it'll be box-office. Whether you knew him in his early days as a confident, charismatic young gun with a pocket full of ambitions and a whole lot more cash, or you first encountered him dismissing an *Apprentice* hopeful with his famous catchphrase, the chances are you were well aware of Trump long before he ran for the biggest job in the world. But behind the bravado, bold statements and love of M&M's, who is the real Trump? Well buckle up, because you're about to find out. From his ancestral roots in rural Germany to his billion-dollar businesses, tumultuous marriages and controversial presidency, we have it all and more. Welcome to the colourful world of the tycoon who may yet shock the globe again this November.

· CONTENTS ·

6
CHAPTER ONE
THE RISE OF THE DON
Inside his ascent from nouveau riche kid to society stalwart and family man

24
CHAPTER TWO
MILLIONAIRES' PLAYGROUND
The Trump brand exudes glitz and glamour, but behind the scenes it hasn't always shone so brightly

40
CHAPTER THREE
YOU'RE FIRED!
Long before he ran for office, Trump was used to calling the shots in TV boardrooms

56
CHAPTER FOUR

SHOCK TO THE SYSTEM

Trump's tumultuous journey to the Oval Office divided America into two committed camps

76
CHAPTER FIVE

CHAOS IN THE CAPITOL

In the wake of his defeat, Trump implored his followers to fight back. Many saw it as a call to arms

92
CHAPTER SIX

THESE DISUNITED STATES

As the nastiest election in living memory looms, the U.S. has rarely been so angry and divided

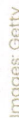

CHAPTER ONE

THE RISE OF THE DON

FROM NOUVEAU RICHE KID TO
SOCIETY STALWART AND FAMILY MAN

• CHAPTER ONE •

"DONALD TRUMP AND HENRY J. HEINZ OF THE HEINZ FOOD COMPANY ARE SECOND COUSINS"

Presidents' ancestors tend to undergo more scrutiny than yours or mine for obvious reasons, and the roots of Donald Trump's family have been traced as far back as the 17th century. Where did those long-gone Trumps live? In rural Germany, of all places, according to research that has isolated a lawyer called Hanns Drumpf as the 45th President's most reliably identifiable ancestor.

Reliable is the key word here: as many an amateur genealogist has found, it's possible to find traces of ancestry even further back than the time period of the late Herr Drumpf, but the problem is that these clues aren't likely to be verifiable. An associated issue is that before about 1800, most of the world's population were agricultural labourers ('ag labs' in family tree slang), recorded only in church records and on grave markers.

Fortunately, Drumpf being a lawyer would have meant that he left a paper trail (a parchment trail?) behind him, and thus we know that he settled in the German village of Kallstadt near Heidelberg in 1608. His offspring changed the family surname to Trump by the middle of the century, and by 1800 the Trumps had established a wine-making business in the Kallstadt area, where Donald's grandfather Friedrich was born in 1869.

Note that a second prominent Kallstadt family, whose surname was Heinz, joined the Trumps by marriage before emigrating to the U.S., where they established the Heinz food company (you probably have a bottle of their famous ketchup in your kitchen). This means that Donald Trump and Henry J. Heinz are second cousins twice removed, although that's a tricky concept to explain.

The Trumps also left Germany for the New World in due course, with Friedrich's son Fred being born in New York in 1905. The family mostly spoke German for the first decade of Fred's life, a fact that he chose to conceal; indeed, he was telling people as late as the 1980s that he was of Swedish rather than German descent. This wariness worked both ways, as a *New York Times* reporter discovered in 2018 on visiting Kallstadt.

"The other Trumps (or 'Droomps', as the name is pronounced in [regional] dialect) listed in a phone book for the area [include] Beate Trump, a podiatrist in another nearby village, for example, or Justin Trump, a teenager whose friends say he sometimes gets teased for his coif of orange-blond hair," ran the article. "But the Weisenborns and the Geissels and the Benders and the Freunds in Kallstadt are related to Mr. Trump, too. 'Practically half the village is,' chuckled Kallstadt's mayor, Thomas Jaworek, before adding, 'I'm not.'"

Fred completed his education in 1923 and, with the financial help of his mother, Elizabeth, established the E. Trump & Son company either one or four years later, depending on which source you consult. The firm's first house was built and sold shortly afterwards, and by 1926 it is thought that 19 more homes had been built in the Queens district of New York – rapid progress by any standards. A step up in the Trump company

This tombstone marks the resting place of some of Donald's ancestors in Kallstadt, Germany

• THE RISE OF THE DON •

Donald's mother, Mary Anne MacLeod, with Donald's older sister Maryanne in 1938

Mary MacLeod Trump and Fred Trump attend the Annual Police Athletic League Awards Dinner in New York, 12 May 1999

A view of Donald's ancestral home of Kallstadt. Tourists enjoy its white wines, hiking trails and the local delicacy – pig's stomach

Donald's father, Fred, pictured in Atlantic City, New Jersey, 22 January 1988

fortunes came in 1934 when they acquired a mortgage-servicing subsidiary of the bankrupt Lehrenkrauss Corporation, enabling Fred to buy a number of houses that were nearing foreclosure and then sell them at a profit.

In 1936, Fred married a Scottish woman seven years his junior called Mary Anne MacLeod. Mary had left the island of Stornoway at the age of 17 for a new life in New York, becoming a U.S. citizen in 1942. The young couple wasted no time when it came to raising a family, producing Maryanne (1937), Fred, Jr. (1938), Elizabeth (1942), Donald (1946) and Robert (1948).

As we go to press in spring 2024, Elizabeth is Donald Trump's last surviving sibling, with Fred, Jr., dying at the age of 42 in 1981, Robert departing in 2020, and Maryanne – who became a senior federal judge – passing away in 2023. In addition, Donald's uncle, Fred's younger brother John G. Trump (1907-1985), was highly respected in the field of physics, developing rotational radiation therapy and receiving Ronald Reagan's National Medal of Science in 1983.

While Mary raised the five children, Fred continued to extend his construction business. In 1938 the *Brooklyn Daily Eagle* newspaper called him "the Henry Ford of the home-building industry," and by 1942 he had constructed 2,000 homes in Brooklyn. He also benefited from federal funds allocated to housing initiatives during World War II, working on large-scale projects involving hundreds of houses for the armed forces.

By the time Donald was born at Jamaica Hospital in Queens on 14 June 1946, the Trump

Picture this: Donald reveals a mid-70s design project to the world, one of many that he worked on under the Trump Organization banner

"I ALWAYS TELL DONALD, 'THE ELEVATOR TO SUCCESS IS OUT OF ORDER. GO ONE STEP AT A TIME'"
FRED TRUMP

Images: Getty

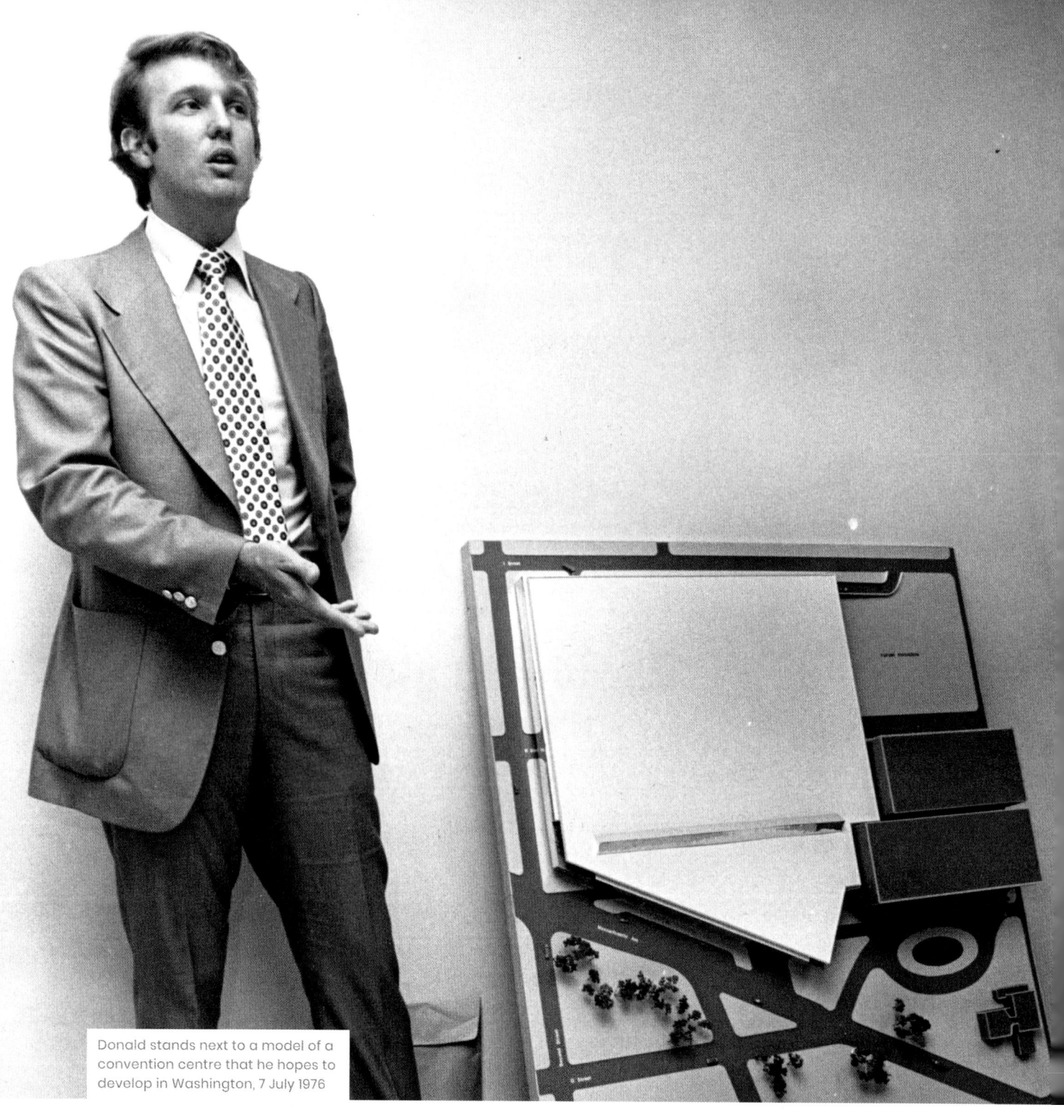

Donald stands next to a model of a convention centre that he hopes to develop in Washington, 7 July 1976

family were both rich and renowned, living in the Jamaica Estates neighbourhood of Queens and able to give their children an elite education. Donald attended a private school called Kew-Forest from kindergarten through seventh grade, transferring to the ominous-sounding New York Military Academy at 13. His academic records have never been published, so we don't know how he performed. We do know that he graduated in 1964 and spent some of his summer vacations working on his father's construction sites.

In 2020, PBS writer Patrice Taddonio wrote an article that implied that Donald's childhood was far from idyllic, quoting *The Art of the Deal* ghostwriter, Tony Schwartz: "I strongly suspect that he had a relationship with his father that accounts for a lot of what he became… and his father was a very brutal guy. He was a tough, hard-driving guy who had very, very little emotional intelligence, to use today's terms." Biographer Timothy O'Brien added: "He said to me that when he arrived at the military academy, for the first time in his life, someone

Mapping it out: Flanked by two architects, Donald points at a model of a proposed convention centre slated to be built over Penn-Central Railroad Yards in New York City, 1975

slapped him in the face when he got out of line… He talks about it as almost this rite of passage."

Yet another author, Gwenda Blair, said of the military schooling: "He loved all that stuff, because it was also really competitive. Other kids didn't like him all that much. He wasn't that popular because he was so competitive… But it was an environment he thrived in. Donald's father's overall message to his children – and it was a very different message to the boys than to the girls – was compete, win, be a killer. Do what you have to do to win."

Trump studied for two years at Fordham University in the Bronx before switching to the Wharton School of Business at the University of Pennsylvania, where he pursued one of the few real estate study courses available at the time. The Vietnam War was raging, with mandatory conscription for young men of sufficient fitness introduced by the U.S. Government. Trump was found fit to serve in 1966 and again two years later, although he was granted a conditional medical deferment in October 1968.

Donald, his mother, Mary, and his wife, Ivana, attend the 38th Annual Horatio Alger Awards Dinner at the Waldorf Hotel, New York, 10 May 1985

He graduated from Wharton School the same year with a Bachelor of Science degree in economics. Looking back at his college years, Donald (or Schwartz) wrote in 1987's *The Art of the Deal* that "perhaps the most important thing I learned at Wharton was not to be overly impressed by academic credentials... In my opinion, that degree doesn't prove very much, but a lot of people I do business with take it very seriously, and it's considered very prestigious. So all things considered, I'm glad I went to Wharton."

It wasn't long before Donald started working for the E. Trump Company, having been encouraged to join the family firm by his father. Initially he worked on building projects in Manhattan, although he also helped out with an Ohio apartment complex and made an investment of $70,000 (about $600,000 today) in a short-lived 1969 Broadway comedy called *Paris Is Out!*

For the sake of a balanced profile, we have to ask the question: was Donald's family wealth responsible for his later success, or did he do the hard work himself? In his later life, Donald claimed that he turned a million-dollar loan from his father into the several billion dollars that he professes to be worth today. It should be noted, however, that an extensive *New York Times* investigation of 2018, stretching to over 100,000 pages of documents, revealed that Donald was being given over a million dollars' worth of untaxed gifts from his father every year by 1968.

An excerpt from the 2018 *NYT* article said: "Mr. Trump won the presidency proclaiming himself a self-made billionaire, and he has long insisted that his father, the legendary New York City builder Fred C. Trump, provided almost no financial help... [our] investigation, based on a vast trove of confidential tax returns and financial records, reveals that Mr. Trump received the equivalent today of at least $413 million from his father's real estate empire, starting when he was a toddler and continuing to this day."

Fred made his son president of his company, which was renamed The Trump Organization, in 1971 when he was 25. He continued to work on large construction projects in Manhattan and elsewhere,

Hair today: Ivana, seen in Paris at a fashion show, met Donald in New York in 1976

In 2014, the Wharton Business School awarded Donald the Joseph Wharton Award

> "HE WORKED FOR THE COMPANY AFTER BEING ENCOURAGED TO JOIN THE FAMILY FIRM BY HIS FATHER"

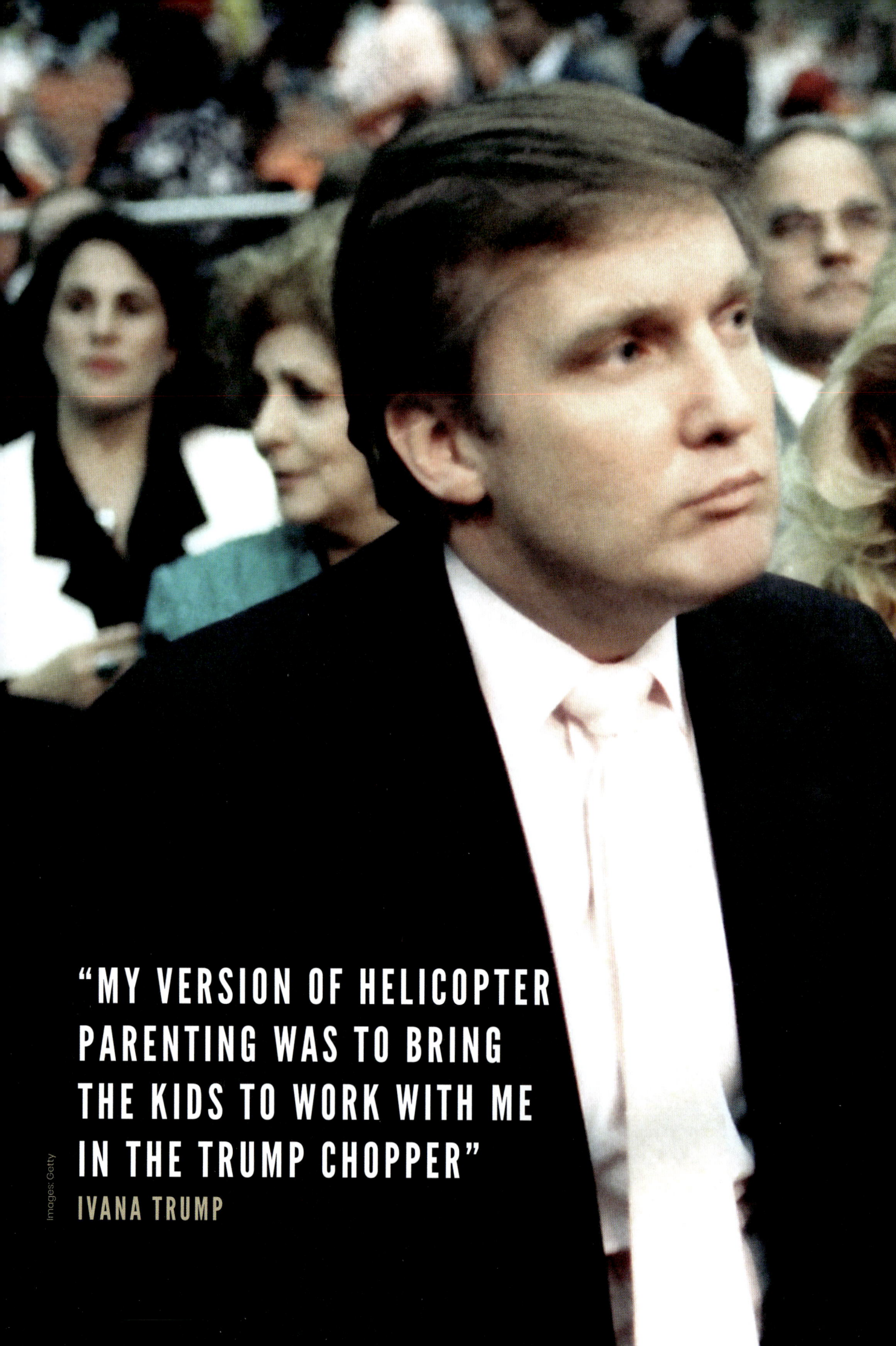

"MY VERSION OF HELICOPTER PARENTING WAS TO BRING THE KIDS TO WORK WITH ME IN THE TRUMP CHOPPER"
IVANA TRUMP

• CHAPTER ONE •

All smiles: Trump and Ivana dressed to the nines in 1982, five years into their marriage

assisted in this by a bone-spur diagnosis that permanently disqualified him from fighting in Vietnam. Early challenges included a 1973 allegation from the Justice Department that the Trump Organization operated in a discriminating fashion against Black tenants, leading to an agreement in which Trump made no admission of wrongdoing.

By the end of '73, the Trump Organization was managing an astonishing 14,000 apartments in Brooklyn, Queens and Staten Island. Over the next couple of years, plans began to be made for the potential construction of the Trump Tower, a project that required a suitable location and an ambitious financing plan. Equally pivotal to the fortunes of the then 30-year-old Donald was a meeting in 1976 with a Czech model named Ivana Marie Zelníčková, who was visiting New York City with colleagues.

As *New York Magazine* wrote in 1990: "Ivana was one of a group of models who came to New York to promote the 1976 Olympic Games in Montreal. Donald Trump spotted her across [high-society bar] Maxwell's Plum and used his pull to get her a table. He was looking for a wife with more character than the Le Club cuties he was used to."

Vanity Fair added the same year: "Maxwell's Plum is gone now, but the very name evokes the era of

"THE TRUMP ORGANIZATION WAS MANAGING AN ASTONISHING 14,000 APARTMENTS"

Donald Trump, Jr., (seated) pictured in 1988 with his parents, Ivana and Donald, at a boxing match between Mike Tyson and Michael Spinks at Trump Plaza in New Jersey

The opera singer Luciano Pavarotti, Ivana Trump, Ivanka Trump and Eric Trump at a party at the Central Park Boathouse in October 1987

Donald and Eric at the US Open tennis tournament at Flushing Meadows Park in New York, 30 August 1991

frantic singles underneath the Art Nouveau ceiling. It was the place where flight attendants hoped to find bankers and models looked for dates. Donald met his model, Ivana Zelníčková, visiting from Montreal."

The same article added that an early trip together ended in embarrassment for Donald: "[Ivana] liked to tell the story of how she had gone skiing with Donald, pretending to be a learner like him, and then humiliated him by whizzing past him down the slopes."

Ivana certainly had character. Born in 1949 in Gottwaldov, Czechoslovakia (now Zlín in the Czech Republic), she was a competitive skier in Austria and Italy by the age of 12, although Soviet-era restrictions meant that travel across the Iron Curtain wasn't easy. She gained a master's degree in physical education in Prague and secured a Western passport after a quickie marriage to an Austrian skier, Alfred Winklmayr, for that exact purpose. Later, she lived in Montreal, Canada, for two years, working as a ski instructor and learning English at college while doing occasional modelling gigs for Eaton's department store and promo work for events such as the one for the 1976 Summer Olympics that had led her to Donald.

Striking up a relationship, Donald and Ivana agreed to marry, signing a prenuptial agreement in March 1977. On this, *Vanity Fair* commented: "Donald had already made his alliance with Roy Cohn, who would become his lawyer and mentor. Shortly before the wedding, Donald reportedly told Ivana, 'You have to sign this agreement.' 'What is this?' she asked. 'Just a document that will protect my family money.' Cohn gallantly offered to find Ivana a lawyer. 'We don't have these documents in Czechoslovakia,' Ivana reportedly said."

Despite this awkward moment, the couple married on 9 April at the Trump family place of worship, the Marble Collegiate Church on Fifth Avenue, in a lavish ceremony presided over by his family pastor, Norman Vincent Peale.

Like Fred and Mary before them, the couple were quick to have children, with Donald, Jr., arriving in December 1977, Ivana Marie – nicknamed "Ivanka" – following in October 1981, and finally Eric in January 1984. According to an article in *Vanity Fair*, Donald always longed for a big brood.

"I'M A REALLY GOOD FATHER... YOU'VE PROBABLY FIGURED OUT MY CHILDREN REALLY LIKE ME – LOVE ME – A LOT"

"Donald was determined to have a large family. 'I want five children, like in my own family, because with five, then I will know that one will be guaranteed to turn out like me,' Donald told a close friend. He was willing to be generous with Ivana, and a story went around that he was giving her a cash bonus of $250,000 for each child."

So what kind of dad was Donald? Not the diapers-changing kind, we know that much. "I don't do that," he said on *Opie and Anthony* in 2005. "There's a lot of women out there that demand that the husband act like the wife and, you know, there's a lot of husbands that listen to that... I'm really like a great father, but certain things you do and certain things you don't. It's just not for me."

"Children are tough. Much tougher than people think," he told *New York Magazine*. "I'm a really good father but not a really good husband. You've probably figured out my children really like me – love me – a lot. It's hard when somebody walks into the living room of Mar-a-Lago in Palm Beach and this is supposed to be, like, a normal life. But they're very grounded and very solid."

As for the perennial dad challenge of balancing family with work, Trump ruminated: "The hardest thing for me about raising kids has been finding the time.

"I know friends who leave their business so they can spend more time with their children, and I say, 'Gimme a break!' My children could not love me more if I spent 15 times more time with them."

CHAPTER TWO

MILLIONAIRES' PLAYGROUND

THE TRUMP BRAND EXUDES GLITZ AND GLAMOUR, BUT BEHIND THE SCENES IT HASN'T ALWAYS SHONE SO BRIGHTLY

• CHAPTER TWO •

What's in a name? For many people across America, Trump is a brand synonymous with the hard-selling, can-do mindset that made America what it is today. Looking at Trump with the benefit of hindsight, it isn't difficult to see how business and politics came together and why Trump might appeal to many Americans.

Over the course of half a century, brand Trump has incorporated many businesses across an unprecedented range of industries. Few corporations have been as far-reaching and keen to expand into new markets. Trump has tried his hand at almost everything, from his more recognised and enduring property interests to more obscure and short-lived endeavours.

Starting his business career at Trump Management, the real-estate company owned and operated by his father, Fred, Donald quickly established personal wealth. This came from deals assisted by financial backing from his father. On becoming president of Trump Management in 1971, Donald renamed the company The Trump Organization, and by 1973 he directed the management of thousands of residential units across three of the five New York Boroughs – Staten Island, Queens and Brooklyn. This was the catalyst for one of his first high-profile controversies when the Justice Department alleged that The Trump Organization was actively discriminating against Black tenants. It was discovered that employees were marking Black people who had made enquiries about renting apartments with a unique code, suggesting they were being profiled based on ethnic background.

Donald and his father called on Roy Cohn, formerly an aide to Senator Joseph McCarthy, to defend their company in the legal proceedings as they prepared to sue the U.S. Government for $100 million in damages. This counterclaim was later dismissed by District Judge Edward R. Neaher. However, despite Black and white test applicants receiving unbalanced approvals for apartment applications in multiple Trump-operated buildings, with Black renters being redirected to other predominantly Black-populated buildings, an

New York City has some of the most profitable real estate in the world

• MILLIONAIRES' PLAYGROUND •

Trump Tower is located at 725 5th Ave, Manhattan, on the former site of the Bonwit Teller Building

During the 1970s, Donald operated up to 14,000 apartments across Staten Island, Queens and Brooklyn

"IT WAS CLEAR THAT TRUMP SAW NEW YORK AS HIS CORPORATE PLAYGROUND"

agreement was reached under which Donald had to offer equal opportunities to all tenants but admitted to no wrongdoing.

From the early days it was clear Trump saw New York as his corporate playground and intended to conquer this competitive property market. His first large acquisition was the ageing and outdated Commodore Hotel, located on the corner of East 42nd Street and Lexington Avenue, one block from the Chrysler Building – a symbol of decadent New York architecture. A complete renovation turned this faded Manhattan high-rise into a shiny glass monolith, the first of several that would soon be emblazoned with Trump titles.

In early 1979, Donald bought the Bonwit Teller flagship store on the eastern side of Fifth Avenue. He had wanted the site for many years, regularly making overtures to the owners for a sale. He got his wish and promptly demolished the existing building, causing some consternation over the loss of such an architecturally significant structure. Opened in October 1929, the 12-storey Bonwit Teller flagship building was a shining example of art-deco design, and its replacement with the Modernist, glass-heavy 58-floor Trump Tower remains an unpopular decision four decades

• CHAPTER TWO •

The Commodore Hotel, now the Grand Hyatt, was one of Donald's first major acquisitions

The Tiffany Co. Building neighbours Trump Tower on 5th Ave, over which Donald purchased the air rights

later. This was made worse by the destruction of several art-deco bass-relief carvings that had proudly adorned the Bonwit Teller Building. These artworks had been destined for preservation in the Metropolitan Museum of Art but were damaged in the hasty tear-down process.

As became a trend with future Trump projects, the construction of the Tower itself attracted controversy, with the alleged use of hundreds of poorly paid illegal Polish migrant workers. A 16-year court battle ensued, which was finally settled in Trump's general favour in 1999.

The project was topped out in 1982 almost $100 million over budget. However, Trump was confident that the Tower's location would pay for itself. One of its neighbours was the Tiffany & Co. flagship store, so it was in good company in a sought-after area of Midtown Manhattan. Not one to be outdone, Trump went as far as purchasing the air rights above the Tiffany Building to prevent any future development of that site that might produce a taller tower. A series of high-profile tenants, including director Steven Spielberg and actress Sophia Loren, quickly offset the cost of construction. Further towers followed, including the Trump International Tower in Chicago – the second-tallest hotel in the city – which in 2010 received the accolade of being the best large-city hotel building in North America.

The 1980s were a time of exciting expansion for Trump, spawning a dizzying level of diversification in his business portfolio. After the construction of Trump Tower and the successful renovation of the Wollman Rink in Central Park several hundred thousand dollars under budget, it was time for Trump to aim even higher. One of his least-known investments, yet perhaps one of his most ambitious, was the launch of his own airline.

In the absence of reliable high-speed rail links up the East Coast of the U.S., air travel had long been

The Wollman Rink in Central Park, which Donald successfully restored to profitability in the 1980s

> "THE WORST THING YOU CAN POSSIBLY DO IN A DEAL IS SEEM DESPERATE TO MAKE IT. THAT MAKES THE OTHER GUY SMELL BLOOD, AND THEN YOU'RE DEAD"
>
> DONALD TRUMP

CHAPTER TWO

a popular solution. The ultra-high flight frequency market was a profitable one and, after Eastern Airlines ran into financial trouble brought on by a bitter strike, its 'shuttle' business arm went up for sale. Feeling it would align with his other property and resort businesses, Trump snapped up the airline for $365 million, inheriting 22 Boeing 727-100/-200 aircraft, and Trump Shuttle was born.

To properly 'Trump-ify' his planes, Donald invested heavily in installing plush cabin features and glitzy embellishments in the hope of differentiating his product from competitors. On 8 June 1989, Trump Shuttle began hourly services between Boston, Washington Regan and New York LaGuardia airports. Trump wasted no time in solidifying the illusion of glamour, claiming that in addition to being the first flight out of LaGuardia, Trump Shuttle was "the most successful" and that he thought it "had better service than anyone else".

Overnight, Trump had almost half of the East Coast shuttle market, which was one of the justifications for the high price he had paid for Eastern. However, despite punctuality being a key selling point of the airline, poor weather delayed the very first rotation from New York to Washington – a portent of things to come.

A series of conflicts in the Middle East forced significant increases in fuel prices, which, combined with a reduction in travellers as a result of an economic downturn, produced the worst-

Donald marks the launch of his Trump Shuttle airline division at the Plaza Hotel, June 1989

case scenario for any airline business model. Losses quickly mounted and, after missing bank loan repayments, Trump Shuttle was sold to USAir. The brand ceased to exist in the spring of 1992, and it was later reported that the business never managed to turn a profit.

Trump Shuttle wasn't the only failed business Donald had invested in, and it seems bankruptcy has never been as far behind him as his outwardly confident demeanour would have the world believe. While Trump has never filed for personal bankruptcy, several of his businesses have, in some cases multiple times. For example, Trump Entertainment Resorts, founded as Trump Hotels and Casino Resorts in 1995, filed for Chapter 11

Bad omen: A Trump Shuttle Boeing 727 after an emergency landing in Boston, 15 August 1989

• MILLIONAIRES' PLAYGROUND •

Donald launches his GoTrump.com luxury travel brand website on 24 January 2006

Trump launched his short-lived vodka brand in 2006. It shut down in 2011

bankruptcy protection at least three times during its history, notably in 2004, 2009 and 2014. The company began with the purchase of multiple entertainment properties along the Atlantic City Boardwalk in New Jersey in the early 1980s. The first to reopen was the Trump Plaza Hotel and Casino, followed by the Atlantic City Hilton Hotel and Casino, which later became the Trump's Castle Hotel Casino.

By the early 2000s, Trump Hotels and Casino Resorts had run into financial challenges and were laden with debt. It filed for bankruptcy in December of 2004, with Donald playing the situation down in his inimitable style as "just a technical thing". The company became Trump Entertainment Resorts thereafter and Donald took a step back from the day-to-day management of operations. By 2009, the company had amassed debts in excess of a billion U.S. dollars and had to enter talks for a bail-out. The next few years saw the sale of Trump Marina to raise funds and, after the 2014 filing, the closure of Trump Plaza.

Many other business ventures Trump has dipped into over the decades have been far from successful. He started up his own brand of vodka in 2006, but this never became a staple of the American licence trade as he would have hoped. This division was shut down in 2011. Furthermore, Trump Steaks was opened in 2007 but lasted only five years before it was closed due to poor health code conformity. The brand was even extended into the luxury travel industry with the launch of

Donald samples his product at the launch of Trump Steaks, New York, 2007

"HE WAS A LARGE PERSONALITY AND OFTEN SEEN MIXING WITH A BROAD RANGE OF CELEBRITIES"

the short-lived GoTrump.com in 2006. Using the slogan "The art of the travel deal" in reference to Donald's autobiography, this venture was aimed at attracting high-end travel clients. However, even Henry Harteveldt, the former marketing director for the Trump Shuttle, referred to the site as a vanity project and cast doubt on the viability of the business. These doubts proved warranted and the website was closed down the following year.

Throughout his business career, Trump has felt the weight of the combined losses of each of his companies, drawing on his ability to create an impression of success to encourage investment from others to support his brand through tough times. He has also made extensive use of Chapter 11 bankruptcy filings, under which his troubled companies have been able to continue trading while Trump negotiated supporting deals. In 2011 he was quoted as saying, "I do play with the bankruptcy laws," describing the policies as "very good for me".

On many occasions, Trump's interpretation of the law has been called into question, which has pitted him against the U.S. Government in – sometimes highly public – disputes. However, his personal life has often proven to be just as dramatic. His three marriages have each drawn much attention, not always for good reasons. While his entertainment businesses soared, he was already a large personality in his own right and was often seen mixing with a broad range of celebrities. While he was married to his first wife, Ivana, he was allegedly engaged in an affair with actress and model Marla

Today known as the Hard Rock Hotel & Casino Atlantic City, the Trump Taj Mahal opened in April 1990 and was marketed as the "eighth wonder of the world"

• CHAPTER TWO •

Maples. The pair had first met in 1984. Following his divorce from Ivana in 1990, Donald and Marla engaged in a highly publicised relationship. They had a daughter, Tiffany, in October of 1993, with Donald proposing later in December of that year. The couple married on 20 December in the Plaza Hotel, Manhattan. The name Tiffany is a direct callback to Trump's obsession with the coveted plot of land on Fifth Avenue, close to where he constructed Trump Tower.

Trump may not seem to promote a sentimental side publicly, but Marla later reported that his decision to propose to her had an external motivation. She claimed that the Long Island Rail Road shooting in December 1993, in which six people were killed, had encouraged Trump to rethink the direction of his life and secure their relationship. He reportedly said, "I figured life is short, and I want to do this now." This does conflict with reports that, upon learning Marla was pregnant with Tiffany, Trump had asked, "What are we going to do about this?", a question many believe was a suggestion she should terminate the pregnancy. Trump avidly denied this.

The first three years of the marriage seemed happy, but a shift in tone occurred in 1996 when Trump dismissed his bodyguard, Spencer Wagner. While this act itself would not indicate anything about the state of his marriage, it was reported that Wagner had been discovered with Marla in a compromising position in a lifeguard stand on an empty Mar-a-Lago beach in the early hours of the morning. Marla and Trump equally denied an affair, as did Wagner, whose bodyguard business failed as a result of the scandal. Wagner's ex-wife, Mary Miller, revealed that he was "crushed" by the suggestion of wrongdoing and that he had found Marla a challenging client to control. Miller does not believe the affair occurred, despite claiming that Marla would – according to Wagner – "try to pull him into a bedroom in the house". Wagner

The relationship between Donald and Marla Maples was followed closely by the press

died of a drug overdose in 2012, never having fully recovered from the public scandal.

Regardless of whether an affair between Marla and Wagner had actually occurred, her relationship with Trump was soon to end. The couple separated in May 1997 and were divorced in June 1999. Despite this very public marital breakdown, Trump's children from each of his marriages seem to maintain a fond relationship. Ivanka assisted Tiffany in achieving an internship at fashion magazine *Vogue* in 2011 and, publicly at least, the two seem to be model sisters navigating the fame that comes with being the daughters of one of the most recognised men on Earth.

Trump's third marriage, this time to Slovenian-American model Melanija Knavs in 2005, was to be different, significant for reasons beyond the public image that is needed to create the impression of stability expected of a high-flying businessman. 'The Don' had plans to take his name to the very top of the American political elite. With his eye on the Oval Office, Melania would serve as his first lady. However, long before he would ever be seen standing behind a podium emblazoned with the presidential seal, Trump would become a TV personality of a different kind, in an environment in which he felt most at home – the boardroom.

"THE COUPLE SEPARATED IN MAY 1997 AND WERE DIVORCED IN JUNE 1999"

Donald and Marla married at the Plaza Hotel in December 1993 in front of more than 1,000 guests

CHAPTER THREE
YOU'RE FIRED!

LONG BEFORE HE RAN FOR OFFICE, TRUMP WAS USED TO CALLING THE SHOTS IN TV BOARDROOMS, PENNING BEST SELLERS AND EVEN FEATURING IN AN R&B VIDEO...

Image: Getty

CHAPTER THREE

Unlike most presidents-elect – in fact, unlike all of them except Ronald Reagan – Trump was widely known to the general public long before he entered office in 2015. This was because he'd been appearing on television and film screens for three decades, often in cameo roles but also through promoting his books and businesses.

For evidence, check out CBS News' 20 January 2017 coverage of what is thought to be Trump's first TV interview – a filmed chat with *60 Minutes* presenter Mike Wallace in 1985. When Wallace asks Trump, "You're in your late 30s. You've got 40 years to live, minimum. What are you going to do?", the future 45th president replies, "Not politics… there are very few really capable people around, and those people do have to go into politics."

Just as he said, Trump chose to pursue a public profile in other ways, firstly by making comedic cameo appearances in television series such as *The Jeffersons* (1985) and *I'll Take Manhattan* ('87). Soon after, he established a lucrative niche as an author. His 1987 book *The Art of the Deal* – credited to him but actually written by his co-author, Tony Schwartz – was a resounding success in and out of the business world, topping the *New York Times* best-seller list and remaining on the list for 48 weeks. Trump then appeared in a bit part in a subpar 1989 film called *Ghosts Can't Do It*, receiving a Golden Raspberry award for his efforts, and in the video clip for R&B singer Bobby Brown's single 'On Our Own' the same year. He even made a surreal appearance on the UK sports programme *Saint and Greavsie* in 1991, drawing the teams for the fifth round of that year's Rumbelows Football League Cup (seriously – it's on YouTube).

Trump's role in 1992's *Home Alone 2: Lost In New York* is the one for which he is best remembered, not because his screen time is very long – he gets about ten seconds to give Macaulay Culkin's lost pre-teen directions in a hotel lobby – but because the movie was such a huge hit. As a way of getting himself in front of millions of viewers, the role was a significant marketing success: Trump followed it up with a string of film and TV appearances through the rest of the decade.

These normally played humorously on his image as a heartless capitalist, whether as a dad who says, "You're the best son money can buy" (*The Little Rascals*, 1994), a house guest sighing, "Everybody blames me for everything" (*The Fresh Prince of Bel-Air*, also '94), a poker player unwilling to risk a quarter (*Suddenly Susan*, '97) or simply a New York high-society figure (*Sex and the City*, '99).

Trump's name continued to appear on books such as *Trump: Surviving at the Top* (1990), *Trump: The Art of the Comeback* (1997) and *The America We Deserve* (2000), in the last of which he switched focus from business to a wider social viewpoint. He also became a regular on the radio show hosted by the politically incorrect DJ Howard Stern, racking up many appearances from 1997 to 2005, and appeared – in non-sexual scenes it should be noted – in *Playboy* video collections released between 1994 and 2001. You even encountered Trump between shows as he appeared in adverts for Pizza Hut and McDonald's, as well as Pepsi, Macy's, Oreos and many other companies.

The 2000s were the decade in which the Trump brand really became disseminated in the media, thanks firstly to cameo roles in *Zoolander* (2001), *Two Weeks Notice* (2002) and – believe it or not – *Da Ali G Show* (2003). The last of these was an instance of pure comedy gold, with the title character attempting to sell his 'ice cream gloves' idea to a dismissive Trump, but the mocking laughs were reduced later the same year with the launch of the production for which he will always be best known: NBC's *The Apprentice*.

> "HE GETS ABOUT TEN SECONDS TO GIVE MACAULAY CULKIN DIRECTIONS IN A HOTEL LOBBY"

YOU'RE FIRED!

Trump pictured in a cameo role in the 1987 CBS television mini-series *I'll Take Manhattan* alongside Valerie Bertinelli, the sometime wife of guitarist Eddie Van Halen

Trump, alongside the journalist Barbara Walters on a private helicopter, filming the 1987 ABC News TV series *20/20*

By the late 1980s Trump was a chat-show regular. Here he is in an interview with TV host David Letterman on 22 December 1987

• CHAPTER THREE •

In 1992, Trump appeared alongside the lead actress Susan Lucci on Disney's *All My Children*, a soap opera that ran from 1970 to 2011

Trump chats with actor Michael Douglas at a Children of Chernobyl Relief Fund event. The pair went on to appear together in 2010's *Wall Street: Money Never Sleeps*

• YOU'RE FIRED! •

You're almost certainly familiar with this show and how it works, whether from the Trump-hosted original that he presented until 2015, or from its British equivalent, launched in 2005 and still hosted by Lord Alan Sugar. Contestants enter the show intending either to work for the host or to go into a business partnership with him and are given a series of money-making tasks to execute. A member of the lowest-scoring team is dismissed from the show each week with the trademark phrase 'You're fired' until only one remains. It's a very watchable experience, with high viewer numbers to match, mostly because you can't help but cringe at the ridiculous arrogance and entitlement of the competitors, as well as their inability to perform simple jobs.

The shows, both American and British, were the idea of a British TV producer called Mark Burnett, who brought Trump on board for a co-production credit and a nominal fee of $50,000 per episode.

Once *The Apprentice* became a hit, however, Trump began to earn much more, with the *New York Times* calculating in 2020 that he eventually earned $427 million from his 11-year, 14-season run as the show's host – $197 million from direct payments and a further $230 million from *Apprentice*-related business.

The on-screen drama soon proliferated. An advisor on *The Apprentice* named Carolyn Kepcher was the COO and general manager for Trump National Golf Club and became famous herself thanks to her screen time: when she was fired both from the show and Trump's organisations – with only the words "I wish her all the best" as a public explanation – the headlines were immediate and widespread. Trump's sons Eric and Donald, Jr., soon took Kepcher's place, on the TV show at least. His wife, Melania, also appeared from time to time, promoting her fashion lines and cosmetics; his daughter Ivanka did the same.

No slapping today: Trump shakes hands with Will Smith, the Fresh Prince of Bel-Air, on the set of the show of the same name

Image: Getty

"JAY LENO AND HIS PEOPLE ARE CONSTANTLY CALLING ME TO GO ON HIS SHOW. MY ANSWER IS ALWAYS NO BECAUSE HIS SHOW SUCKS. THEY LOVE MY RATINGS!"

DONALD TRUMP

• CHAPTER THREE •

Two spinoff series duly appeared: *The Celebrity Apprentice* (2008) and *The Ultimate Merger* (2010). On the former, well-known personalities competed to raise money for charity; on the latter, entrants competed to go on a date with a former political consultant called Omarosa Onee Newman, who had appeared on the first season of *The Apprentice*. A third spinoff titled *The Apprentice: Martha Stewart* was hosted by the titular lifestyle guru in 2005.

The Apprentice came to an end, at least for Trump, in 2015: NBC fired him after he made some comments about Mexican immigrants in his announcement that he was running for the White House. A further season was hosted by the former California governor Arnold Schwarzenegger in 2017, a short-lived project despite the on-screen charisma of the Austrian Oak.

It was reported that producer Burnett continued to pitch *Apprentice*-themed ideas to Trump after his election as president, including a show supposedly named *The Apprentice: White House*. The idea, it's said, was that the show would take

Trump poses for the cameras after signing a poster depicting the cover of his new book, New York, 2004

place after Trump was replaced in office, rather than while he was the sitting head of state. However, the idea has never materialised.

In between shooting episodes of *The Apprentice*, Trump kept busy with the occasional cameo role in film and TV, making his name and face inseparable from his business. He appeared on Saturday Night Live in 2004, on *Days of Our*

Poster boy: A banner promoting *The Apprentice* hangs from the entrance of Trump Tower, 2004

YOU'RE FIRED!

With Melania and a young fan at a party for *The Apprentice* in West Hollywood, California, 26 February 2004

Thumbs up: The winning competitor Bill Rancic poses with Trump at *The Apprentice* finale viewing party at Trump Tower, 15 April 2004

Lives in 2005, and in a couple of truly unexpected wrestling-related shows – *WWE Raw* and *WrestleMania 23* – in 2007 and 2009. In the former he played out a skit in which he 'bought' the WWE Raw brand; in the latter he announced a spoof 'Battle of the Billionaires' match with the wrestling mogul Vince McMahon.

None of this was supposed to be taken seriously, and all of it was highly watchable car-crash TV, but Trump sailed impassively through it, agreeing to be roasted on the Comedy Central Roast in 2011, hosting a Discovery Channel documentary the same year called 'What's America Worth?' and playing his *Apprentice* role in a 2012 episode of *Top Gear* in which the car-loving hosts pitched him a business idea.

Along the way he hosted a talk-radio spot called *Trumped!* from 2004 to 2008 and was a commentator on the Fox news programme *Fox & Friends* from 2011 until his presidential campaign began four years later. Make a point of checking

"NONE OF THIS WAS TO BE TAKEN SERIOUSLY... IT WAS HIGHLY WATCHABLE CAR-CRASH TV"

out his cameo in *Wall Street: Money Never Sleeps* from 2010: the scene in which he and his fictional counterpart Gordon Gekko, played by Michael Douglas, exchange barbs over business plans is unexpectedly convincing.

Meanwhile, the books kept coming, with 15 more volumes published between 2004 and 2015, when

Taking the cake (from left): Rick Hilton, Mark Burnett, Conrad Hilton, Donald and Melania Trump and Kathy Hilton attend a party for *The Apprentice* in Holmby Hills, California, in 2004

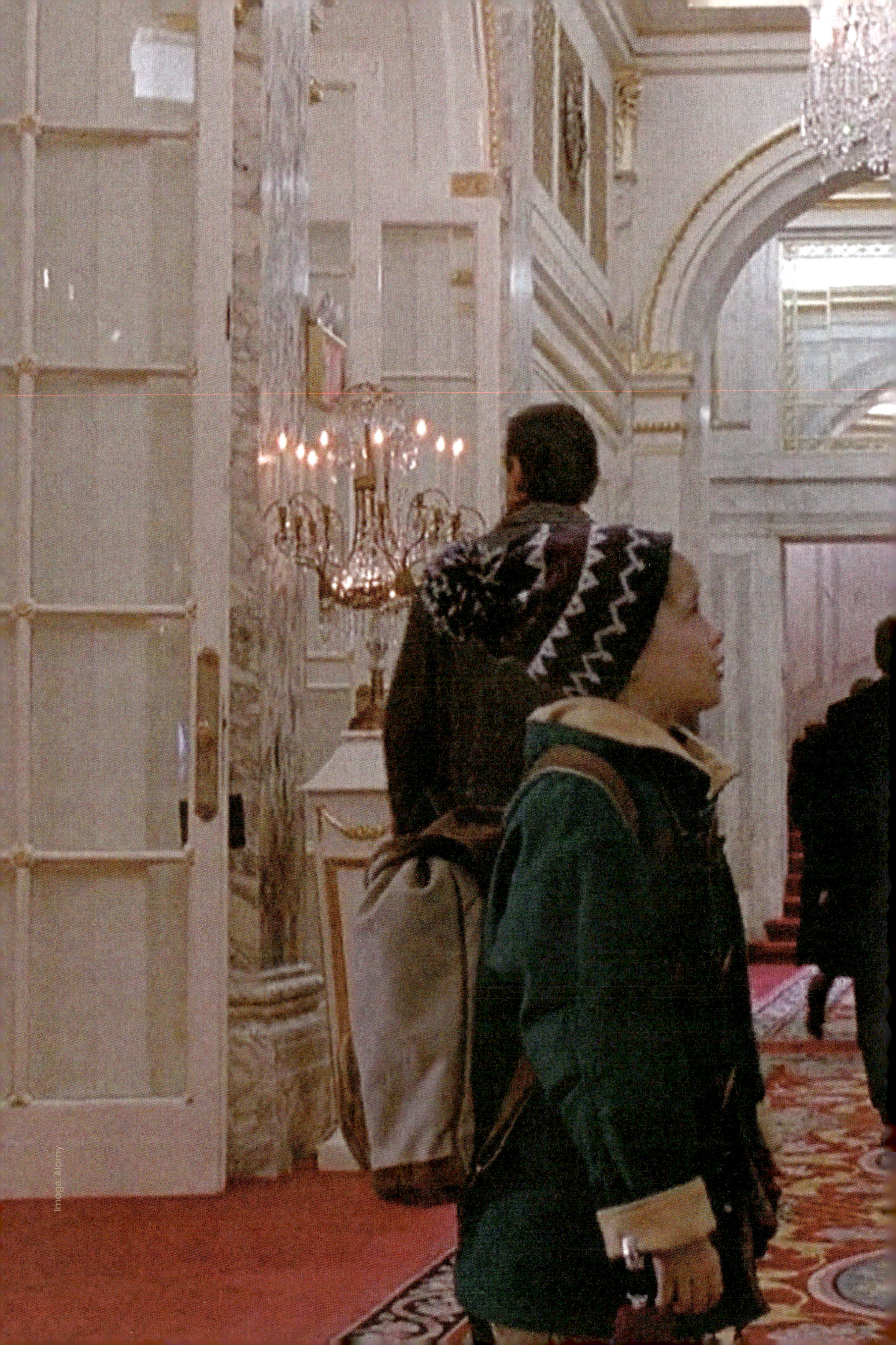
Image: Alamy

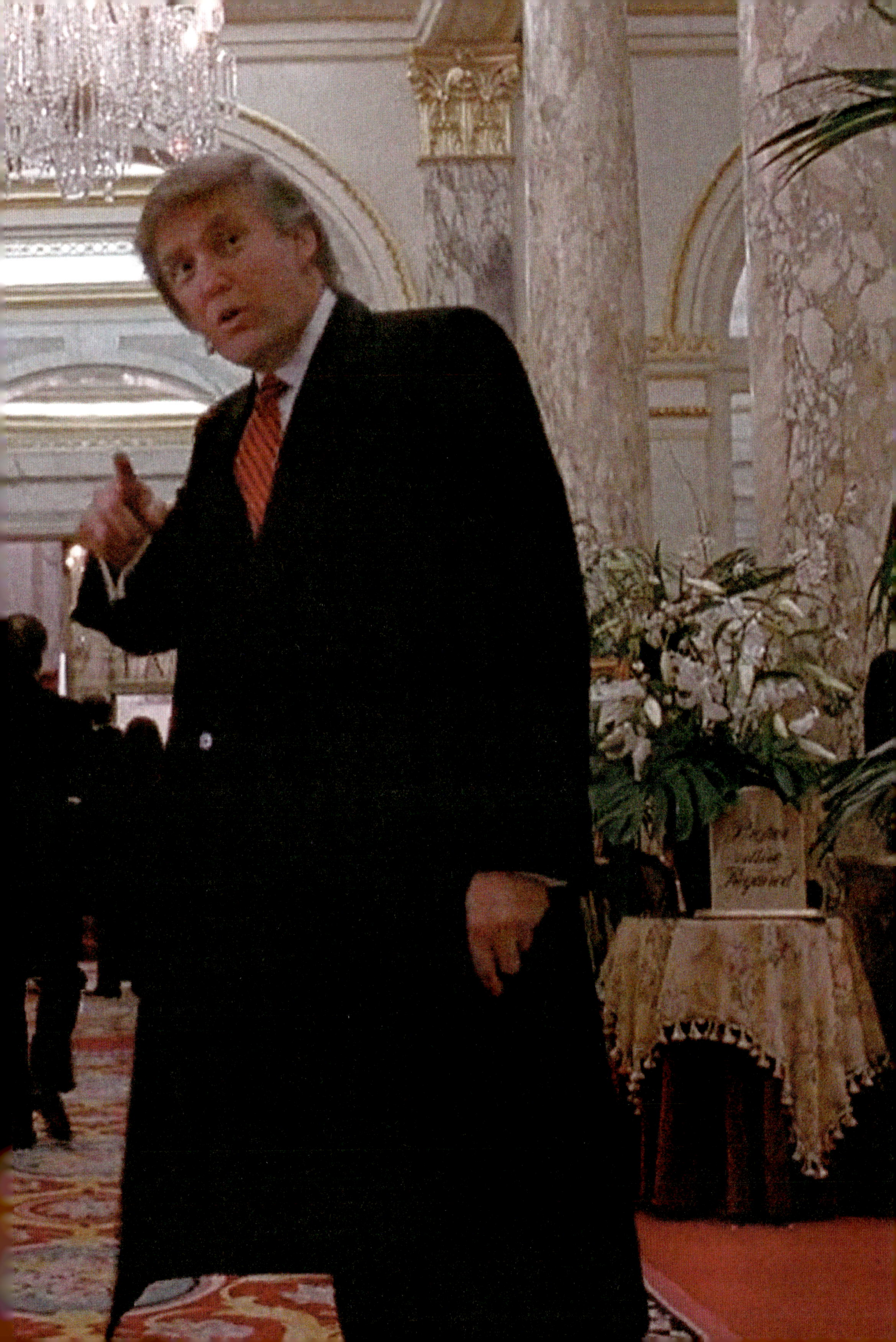

• CHAPTER THREE •

presidential matters began to demand more of Trump's time. These ranged from the simple (*How to Get Rich*, 2004; *Think Big and Kick Ass*, 2007) to the surreal (a novel titled *Trump Tower* that was ghosted by Jeffrey Robinson in 2011), but all of them were about one thing: making money. Of these, the most applicable would appear to be *How to Build a Fortune: Your Plan for Success from the World's Most Famous Businessman*, and *The Best Real Estate Advice I Ever Received: 100 Top Experts Share Their Strategies*, both from 2006, although sports fans might also benefit from *The Best Golf Advice I Ever Received* (2005).

Note that Trump appeared to have leadership on his mind as early as 2011 with a book called *Time To Get Tough: Making America #1 Again*, an ambition that became self-evident four years later with another called *Crippled America: How to Make America Great Again*. With the benefit of hindsight, perhaps Trump's three decades of exposure in all of the above media was executed with one thing in mind: becoming a recognisable, and thus more electable, figure.

You know when a show is a hit in America: *Saturday Night Live* spoofs it. From left: Amy Poehler, Lorne Michaels, Jimmy Fallon, Finesse Mitchell and Trump

"TRUMP APPEARED TO HAVE LEADERSHIP IN MIND IN 2011 WITH HIS BOOK *TIME TO GET TOUGH: MAKING AMERICA #1 AGAIN*"

Trump and his daughter Ivanka pass judgement on *Celebrity Apprentice* in 2010: will they hire or fire?

The *Celebrity Apprentice All Stars* press event in 2012, featuring Trump, his sons Eric and Donald, Jr., – and Gary 'Point Break' Busey, oddly

Arnold Schwarzenegger, seen here about to replace Trump on *The Apprentice* in 2017, gives a speech in San Francisco containing some pointed barbs about his boardroom predecessor

CHAPTER FOUR

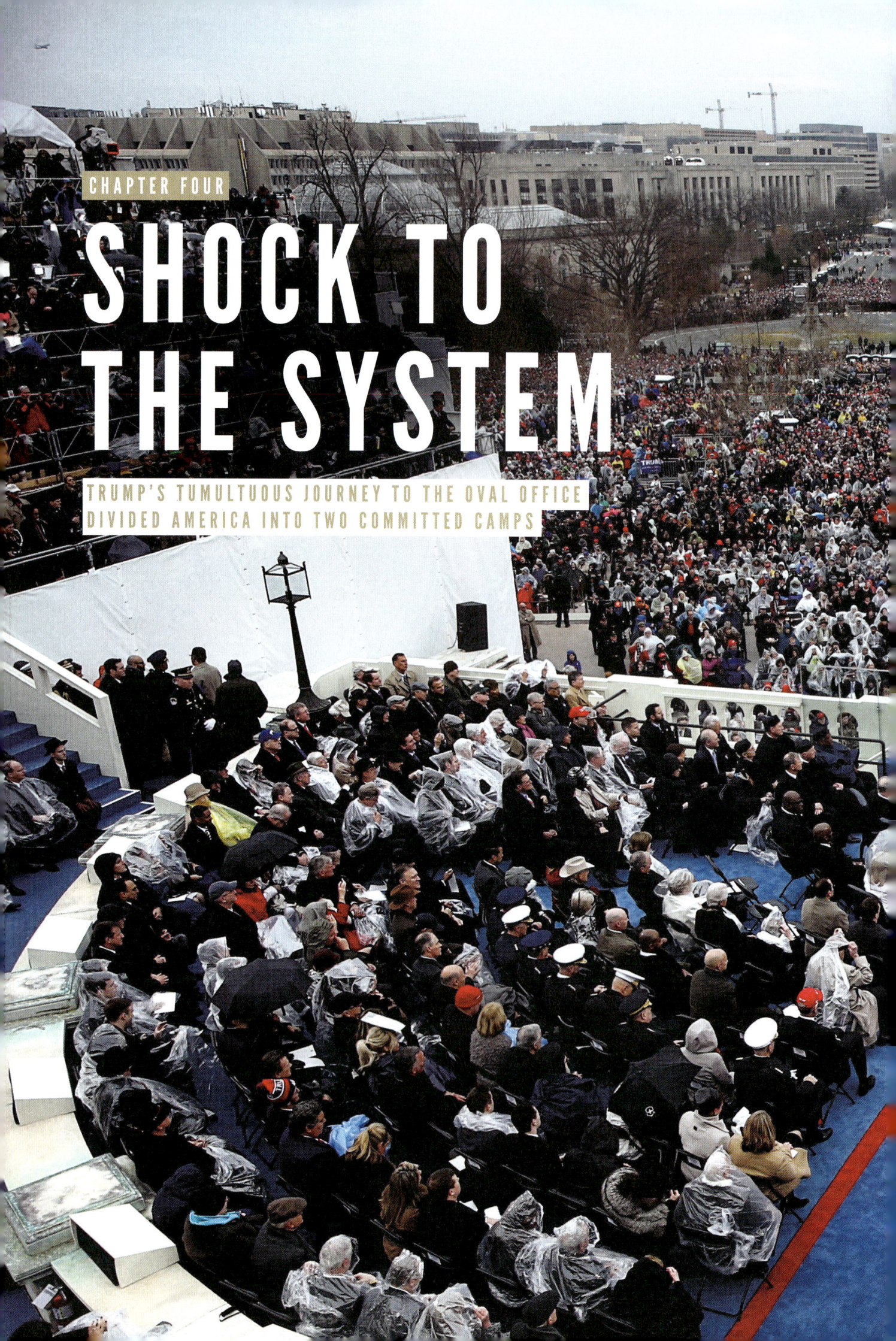

SHOCK TO THE SYSTEM

TRUMP'S TUMULTUOUS JOURNEY TO THE OVAL OFFICE
DIVIDED AMERICA INTO TWO COMMITTED CAMPS

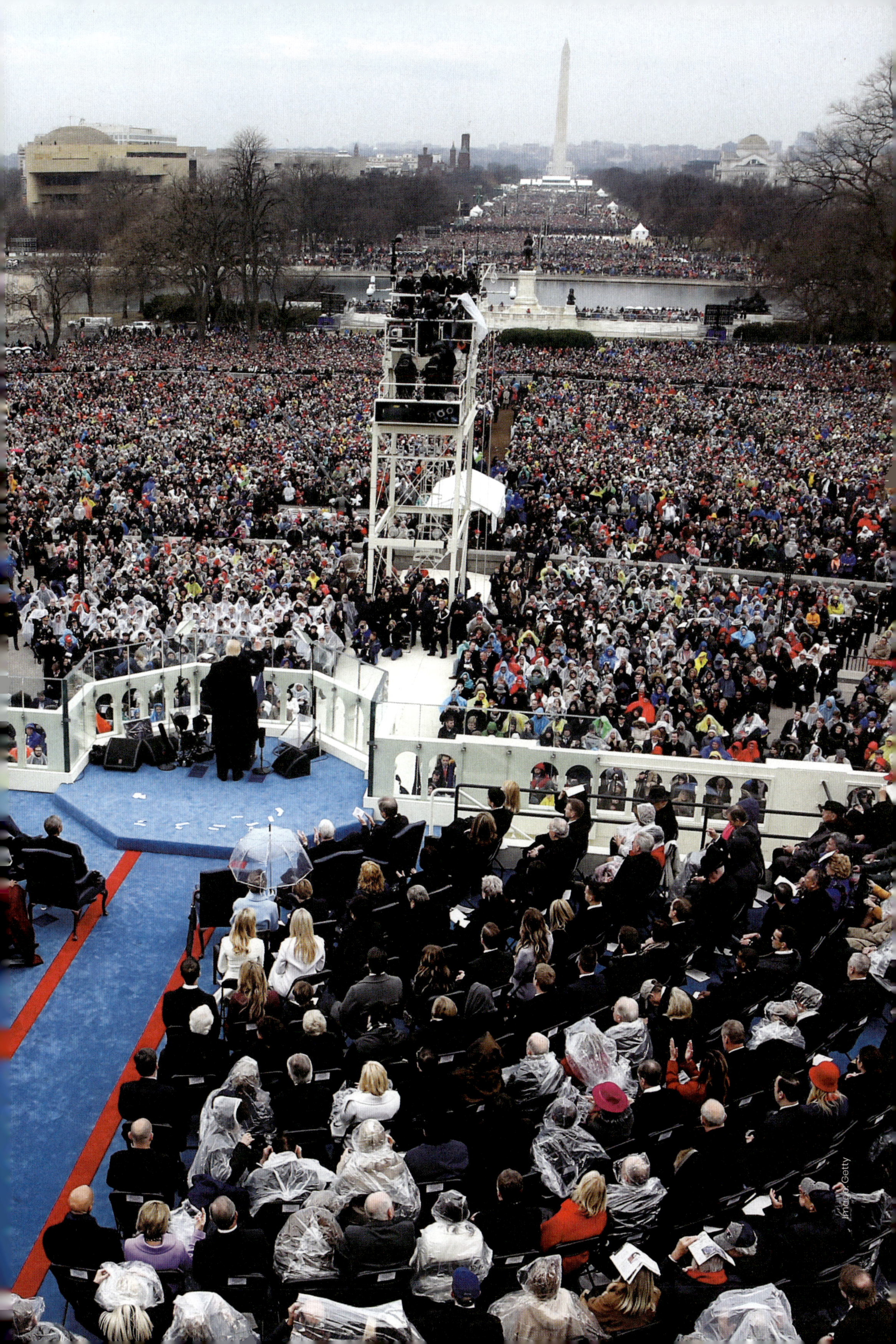
Image: Getty

• CHAPTER FOUR •

On 19 March 2000, the ever-popular animated comedy series *The Simpsons* aired an episode entitled 'Bart to the Future' as part of the show's eleventh season. In the story, a future United States was depicted emerging from a Donald Trump presidential administration. At the time this was predominantly a gag, the character of (President) Lisa Simpson remarking, "We've inherited quite a budget crunch from President Trump." However, the writer of the episode, Dan Greaney, later stated that the decision to work this aspect into the story was "a warning to America," and that, despite the humorous setting, "It was pitched because it was consistent with the vision of America going insane." Fifteen years later, the throwaway line in a cartoon sitcom would be seen by many fans of the show as quite prophetic.

The idea of Donald Trump as president was not an entirely new one, however. As early as 1988, Trump's name had been passed around as a potential candidate for office, a trend that became a staple of multiple elections thereafter. In 1987, Mike Dunbar, a political organiser, pushed Trump forward as an alternative to the lineup of 1988 presidential candidates. While Trump was a Democrat at the time, Dunbar had suggested that he take up a speaking engagement at a Republican candidate conference in New Hampshire. Trump agreed and later that year re-registered himself as a Republican Party member.

Trump's allegiances wavered in the intervening period between the first suggestion of his eligibility and his official 2016 campaign announcement. In late 1999, he became a self-declared candidate for the Reform Party, but by 2001 he had returned to the embrace of the Democrats, stating, "In many cases, I probably identify more as Democrat," and, "It just seems that the economy does better under the Democrats than the Republicans." He even revealed his public support for his later rival Hillary Clinton: "Hillary's always surrounded herself with very good people. I think Hillary would do a good job." However, by September 2009, Trump was once again a Republican Party member, distancing

Protests were held across the world following Trump's successful presidential campaign

• SHOCK TO THE SYSTEM •

Trump's leadership style and policy focus were in stark contrast to outgoing President Obama's

• CHAPTER FOUR •

The debates between Trump and Clinton were often very heated and at times felt intensely personal

Democratic candidate Hillary Clinton already had considerable political experience – an apparent advantage over Trump

himself once more in December 2011 and returning yet again to the GOP (Grand Old Party) fold in 2012.

By 2010, speculation was already rife that Trump would run for the 2012 election. An alleged poll of residents of New Hampshire conducted to gauge popular opinion of Trump added fuel to the media fire, not least because of the mystery surrounding the author of the poll itself. Trump dismissed claims he was behind it: "I never heard of this poll but I'm anxious to find out what it says. I do not know about a poll taken in New Hampshire." He remarked that he did not intend to run for the Republican candidacy but went on to state that "somebody has to do something or this country is not going to be a very great country for long," foreshadowing the slogan he would use for his 2016 campaign.

On 16 June 2015, after more than two decades of flirtation with a political career, the day finally arrived for Trump to officially announce his intention to run for office. This was done in typically Trumpesque fashion, with his descending a golden escalator in Trump Tower to waiting press and spectators. The now-infamous moment – in the eyes of critics – already set the tone for Trump's presidency. "Wow. Woah. That is some group of people. Thousands!" he beamed with a hint of exaggeration as he stepped onto a stage. Those in attendance later reported the true number was closer to a few hundred.

This playfulness with the truth was not what made 16 June a controversial start for the Trump campaign, however. Rather it was the speech Trump then delivered that immediately divided opinion. It was heavily weighted towards highlighting problems with immigration into the United States, namely from Mexico, on which Trump said: "They're sending people that have lots of problems, and they're bringing those problems… They're bringing drugs. They're bringing crime. They're rapists."

Trump waves to the crowds after becoming the 45th president of the United States

Images: Getty

TEXT TRUMP TO 88022
PROMISES KEPT
4 MORE YEARS!
MAKE AMERICA
TRUMP

CHAPTER FOUR

The reaction was justifiably a mixed one. For many years, Trump's views had been called into question, and he made no secret of his negative opinion of President Barack Obama. Trump's announcement speech seemed too radical for even some of his supporters and fellow Republicans. The Republican Party had for some time attempted to appeal more strongly to Hispanic voters, who were the largest minority in the country and overwhelmingly Democrat. Charlotte Alter, a journalist who attended the event on Fifth Avenue, later recalled, "I don't think anybody came away from that announcement thinking he was going to be the next president."

Soon after his June announcement Trump was attending rallies in California, Arizona and Nevada. He even planned to visit the Mexican border, claiming to be putting himself in "great danger". Despite this and his previous comments, Trump insisted that he had a "great relationship" with Hispanic communities. However, this meeting did not take place as a local border patrol union distanced itself from events attended by Trump.

In an article in the San Francisco Chronicle, Mexico's secretary of state José Antonio Meade Kuribreña expressed his concerns about Trump's motives, saying that his views were "coloured by prejudice, racism — or just plain ignorance". He went on to say that such views "have no place in politics". Even fellow Republicans, namely Jeb Bush, who was up against Trump for leadership of the party, publicly criticised him for his comments, highlighting that they did not reflect the views of the party as a whole.

However, there was support for Trump from the Hispanic community, possibly in response to his pledge to repatriate American jobs in a range of industries. While some met Trump at the airport in Laredo with signs bearing slogans of protest, others held placards saying that they were not offended by his remarks.

Trump himself was not entirely committed to the Republicans in the early stages of his campaign and hinted at the possibility of running as an independent candidate. This caused a fiery exchange with other GOP candidates at the Republican primaries, who accused Trump of "hedging his bets". Kentucky Senator Rand Paul levelled that "he's already hedging his bets because he's used to buying politicians" when Trump refused to pledge his support for whomever became the GOP nominee if it wasn't him.

Trump did come under financial pressure for his initial stance on immigration. Several companies cut ties with him commercially, namely Macy's, which announced it would no longer stock Trump-branded products, and Univision, which stopped broadcasting the Trump-operated Miss USA Pageant. Trump sued Univision Communications for $500 million, arguing that this financial pressure was a breach of his First Amendment right to free speech. The matter was latter settled privately.

Trump spoke passionately at his rallies at all stages of his campaign, starting in Manchester, New Hampshire, in front of a crowd of only 300 attendees, through to Mobile, Alabama, which drew crowds of up to 30,000 people. During a speech at the Phoenix Convention Center in Arizona on 11 July 2015, Trump referred to the "silent majority" concept popularised by former president Richard Nixon. This postulated that there existed a large group of people who possessed views aligned with his policies but who didn't express these views publicly. He also called for his supporters to help him "drain the swamp," another catchphrase introduced to the masses by a former president, this time Ronald Reagan. The phrase, which references the historic act

> ## "I DON'T THINK ANYBODY CAME AWAY THINKING HE WAS GOING TO BE THE NEXT PRESIDENT"
> **CHARLOTTE ALTER, TIME MAGAZINE**

• SHOCK TO THE SYSTEM •

Trump announces his intention to run for president at Trump Tower, 16 June 2015

Trump converses with Japanese prime minister Shinzo Abe at a G20 summit hosted in Osaka in 2019

CHAPTER FOUR

of physically draining waterlogged terrain to reduce the spread of malarial infections, was used in American politics as a call to clean out the bureaucracy of former governments.

Campaign events became known for a variety of chants and slogans referencing the wall Trump promised to build along the Mexican border. This inevitably caused friction between his supporters and those protesting his views. Trump was called out for not discouraging violence but also for seemingly inciting aggression on multiple occasions, at least from the point of view of critics. He notably said, "Get 'em out, but don't hurt 'em," about protesters, but at later rallies he encouraged his supporters to "knock the crap out" of some tomato-throwers, going as far as offering to cover any legal fees that might ensue.

Trump secured the role of Republican presidential nominee in July 2016. Having stated throughout the primaries that the system for selecting a nominee was rigged, he promptly reversed his position: "You've been hearing me say it's a rigged system, but now I don't say it anymore because I won. It's true. Now I don't care."

Trump wasted little time in announcing Mike Pence as his running mate and selection for vice president and brought in Kellyanne Conway, an experienced GOP strategist, as campaign manager, predominantly for her advice on how Trump might appeal more strongly to female voters. With this appointment, Conway became the first female Republican general election presidential campaign manager in history.

With his team assembled, the Trump campaign got underway. His opponent, Hillary Clinton, already had a political pedigree that made her a formidable adversary. The former first lady clashed with Trump in the first of three presidential debates on 29 September 2016 at Hofstra University in Hempstead, New York. After a cordial beginning in

Trump on the campaign trail in the early stages of the Republican primaries

which Clinton opted to refer to her opponent as Donald and Trump checked she was happy to be called 'Secretary Clinton', things rapidly became hostile. "You've been doing this for 30 years. Why are you just thinking about these solutions right now?" asked Trump. When he was later pushed to publish his tax returns, Trump said he would "when she releases her 33,000 emails that have been deleted," a direct reference to emails Clinton sent using a private server during her time as secretary of state. Clinton shot back by accusing Trump of being under prepared for their debate. In response to his suggestion that she "stayed at home" while he was out on the campaign trail, Clinton said, "I think Donald just criticized me for preparing for this debate. And yes, I did. And you know what else I prepared for? I prepared to be president."

Trump was forced against the railings on a number of his statements, having to reiterate his position on race and policing. His early run-in with the Justice Department over the profiling of Black residents in his apartments came back to haunt him, with Clinton accusing him of having "a long record of engaging in racist behaviour".

In response, at the second debate in St. Louis, Missouri, Trump made a notable effort to appeal to minority voters. "I want to do things that haven't been done, including fixing and making our inner cities better for the African-American citizens that are so great, and for the Latinos, Hispanics."

Having been called out on his proposed stop-and-search policing strategy, Trump also made a point of how he intended to make this work. "We have to bring back respect to law enforcement. At the same time, we have to take care of people on all sides. We need justice."

The Missouri debate stirred emotions with a question about a tape in which Trump was heard talking about his sexual exploits. Moderator Anderson Cooper grilled him on his unfiltered

The proposed Mexican border wall proved a thorny subject throughout Trump's presidency

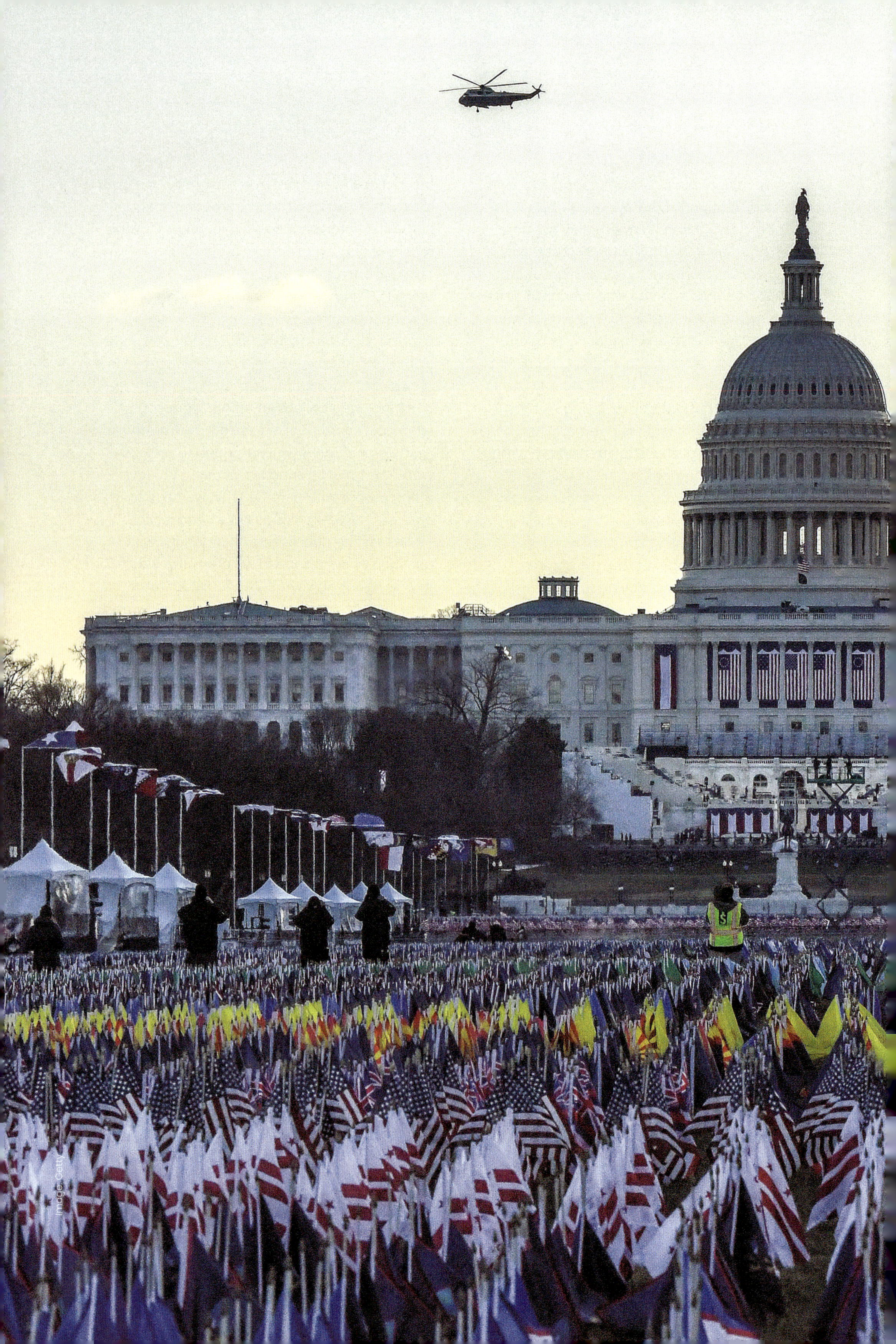

"I DON'T WANT TO BE PRESIDENT. I'M 100 PER CENT SURE. I'D CHANGE MY MIND ONLY IF I SAW THIS COUNTRY CONTINUE TO GO DOWN THE TUBES"

DONALD TRUMP IN 1990

CHAPTER FOUR

– and to many, misogynistic – comments. "You described kissing women without consent, grabbing their genitals. That is sexual assault. You bragged that you have sexually assaulted women. Do you understand that?"

Trump responded by denying that was what he had said and suggesting he had been misunderstood. "No, I didn't say that at all. I don't think you understood what was said. This was locker room talk. I'm not proud of it. I apologise to my family, I apologise to the American people…. I have great respect for women."

Clinton didn't miss the opportunity to respond. "With prior Republican nominees for president, I disagreed with them on politics, policies, principles, but I never questioned their fitness to serve. Donald Trump is different. I said starting back in June that he was not fit to be president…"

When pressed to apologise again for the recording, Trump turned on Clinton: "I think the thing you should be apologising for are the 33,000 emails you acid washed… I hate to say it, but if I win, I am going to instruct my attorney general to get a special prosecutor to look into your situation… Because there has never been so many lies, so much deception."

Later, when Clinton proclaimed, "It's just awfully good that someone with the temperament of Donald Trump is not in charge of the law in our country," Trump instantly hit back "because you'd be in jail".

Their final battle was held at the University of Nevada in Las Vegas on 19 October. Moderated by Fox News anchor Chris Wallace, the debate largely focused on policy over personal attacks. Nevertheless, it was still a tempestuous debate between increasingly bitter rivals.

Asked about his promise to stop migrants from Mexico entering the United States, Trump said: "We're going to secure the border, and once the border is secured – at a later date – we will make a determination as to the rest. But we've got some bad hombres here, and we're gonna get 'em out."

Clinton later called on Trump to denounce Russian president Vladimir Putin and reject Russian support during the run-up to the election.

"I don't know Putin," said Trump with that familiar open-handed gesture. "He said nice things about me. If we get along well that would be good. If Russia and the United States got along well and went after ISIS, that would be good." Pointing to Clinton, he finished the exchange by stating that the Russian leader had no respect "for this person".

Arguably one of the most pressing matters discussed in Sin City was international security, with the former secretary of state accusing Trump of encouraging other nations to acquire nuclear weapons. "All I said was we need to renegotiate these agreements," came Trump's passionate rebuttal, "because our country cannot afford to defend Saudi Arabia, Japan, Germany, South Korea… She took that to mean nuclear weapons. Look, she's been proven to be a liar."

Proving to be as box-office as ever, Trump's most startling reply of the night came when host Wallace asked him whether he would commit to the result of the election. "I will look at it at the time… I will tell you at the time. I'll keep you in suspense." He later told a crowd at a rally in Ohio that he would accept the result "if I win".

Ultimately, controversy turned out to be a powerful tool for Trump, who appealed to the most extremely polarised voters, almost playing on his caricature. Even so, few political commentators gave Trump any hope of victory; the highly regarded website FiveThirtyEight, which tracks opinion polls, politics and economics, among other subjects, calculated that his chance of winning the election was 28.6 per cent. So it came as quite the surprise when, in the early hours of 9 November 2016, Donald Trump was announced as president-elect to a shocked world after securing the 270

"PUTIN SAID NICE THINGS ABOUT ME. IF WE GET ALONG WELL THAT WOULD BE GOOD"

TRUMP
PENCE
MAKE AMERICA GREAT AGAIN!
2020

Trump hired Kellyanne Conway as his senior advisor in a bid to attract more female voters

Trump registers as a New Hampshire Republican primary candidate in November 2015

• CHAPTER FOUR •

Electoral College votes required to win (he would finish with 306 to Clinton's 232).

As a chorus of "USA! USA!" erupted, Trump gave his victory speech in New York, a state that had overwhelmingly voted for Clinton. "Sorry to keep you waiting. Complicated business." After thanking the crowd, he announced, "I've just received a call from Secretary Clinton. She congratulated us – it's about us – on our victory, and I congratulated her on a very hard-fought campaign."

Evidently in a conciliatory mood, Trump reminded America of the debt it owed Clinton for her service before calling on Americans of all political stripes to unite. "Now it's time for America to bind the wounds. We have to get together."

Leaders around the world sent their congratulations and invited Trump for talks. Donald Tusk, president of the European Council, and Jean-Claude Juncker, president of the European Commission, sent a joint letter stating that "it is more important than ever to strengthen transatlantic relations."

For his part, Vladimir Putin expressed his hopes of improving Russia-U.S. relations, having previously expressed personal respect for Trump, calling him a "colourful, talented person".

Unsurprisingly, while he congratulated the U.S. generally, Mexican president Enrique Peña Nieto failed to offer his goodwill to Trump. In the aftermath of the election the value of the Mexican peso plummeted, likely as a result of Trump's disdain for the North American Free Trade Agreement, which had led to successful trade between the U.S. and Mexico. Flor Aguilera, a Mexican writer, bewailed the result to *The Guardian*: "We have been humiliated in front of the world."

Trump's inauguration was held on 20 January 2017. In his seventeen-minute address, he outlined his 'America First' approach, which would ultimately result in him making what some viewed as alarming decisions throughout his presidency without consulting America's traditional allies.

As part of his zero-tolerance initiative to dissuade illegal immigration, in April 2018 Trump introduced the family separation policy for illegal migrants, which ordered that parents be separated from their children once apprehended. In June 2018 it was revealed that the policy did not incorporate any measures to reunite families afterwards, and many are still waiting to be reconnected.

Other divisive policies that Trump implemented included proposed long-term arms deals with Saudi Arabia, valued initially at over $400 billion, and the refusal of entry to the United States to people from Muslim-majority nations.

It was widely reported in the media that Trump's outspoken nature, especially on Twitter, coupled with his tendency to make misleading statements that were later dispelled by qualified fact-checkers, made the White House a sometimes

• SHOCK TO THE SYSTEM •

Trump reversed his family separation policy by signing an executive order in the Oval Office on 20 June 2018

uncomfortable place to be. According to sources reporting to *Time Magazine*, Trump would allegedly become irritated in his presidential briefings if information was brought to his attention that did not align with what he had said in public addresses. It is said Trump would spend several hours a day watching the general media on TV and react to this information more strongly than intelligence from the professional information-gathering community.

Other related differences in his leadership style from former presidents were his preference to receive oral briefings rather than read his President's Daily Brief and the alleged difficulty his staff had in keeping his attention. According to sources, people briefing President Trump would need to use his title and name frequently to ensure focused meetings. This may be one factor in explaining the notably high staff turnover in his cabinet compared to previous administrations.

Trump's domestic policies were met with mixed responses. His reduced support for low-income households, increased trade tariffs on imported goods (which ultimately triggered a trade war with the affected nations) and reduced funding for the agricultural sector were criticised by

• CHAPTER FOUR •

First Lady Melania maintained a relatively low-key presence during her stay at the White House

Trump's first impeachment centered around his request to Ukrainian president Volodymyr Zelenskyy to investigate the Bidens

many, as was his apparent indifference towards regulating police brutality and introduction of funding cuts for local law enforcement agencies. However, it was his stance on climate change and reduced support for environmental protection and sustainable energy that caused the most outrage, particularly his decision to withdraw America from the 2015 Paris Agreement, an international treaty drawn up to contain global temperatures.

Yet while his detractors were many and vocal, Trump achieved several political successes during his presidency. In 2018, he proposed an ambitious audit of the Defence Department to make it easier for citizens to track spending. Thousands of accountants collected and audited 40,000 defence financial documents, revealing areas to improve efficiency and increase spending accountability. A drop in unemployment, wage rises for low-income earners, and making research into Artificial Intelligence a national priority were all achieved on his watch too.

Trump also broke ground on the geopolitical front by becoming the first U.S. president to enter North Korea when he stepped over the demarcation zone from South Korea to shake Kim Jong Un's hand. Speaking through an interpreter, the North Korean leader praised Trump's "courageous and determined act".

Unfortunately for Trump, discussions with another world leader would come back to haunt him when he became only the third U.S. president in history to be impeached. The matter centred around a scandal in which Trump was accused of attempting to coerce newly elected Ukrainian president Volodymyr Zelenskyy into looking into why an investigation in Ukraine into the business dealings of Joe Biden's son Hunter (who had served on the board of a Ukrainian gas company) had suddenly been called to a halt. It was alleged that prior to a 30-minute phone call with Zelenskyy on 21 April 2019, Trump blocked a $391-million military aid package destined for Ukraine in order to push Zelenskyy into reopening the investigation with the hope of him unearthing something that Trump could use to discredit his future political opponent before the 2020 election. On 18 December, two articles of impeachment were issued: Abuse of power and Obstruction of Congress. Trump promised a "complete, fully declassified and unredacted transcript" that would prove his call with Zelenskyy was appropriate and didn't abuse the power of the office, but only incomplete notes of the meeting were released.

This stirred up discussion once again over Trump's previous ties to Russia during his 2016 campaign. Bill Taylor, who served as an ambassador to Ukraine, informed the enquiry that Trump had made investigation into Joe and Hunter Biden a condition of the aid package. It was an explosive testimony, but ultimately it did not prove costly to Trump, who, after a fortnight-long trial, was cleared of the charges.

Heading into the election year, Trump's focus was firmly on beating Biden, but he was soon forced to shift his priorities when the horrifying scale of the Covid-19 pandemic became clear. As deaths mounted and economies crashed across the globe, Trump's administration pumped over $6 trillion into relief efforts designed to shore up U.S. markets and roll out vaccines efficiently through Operation Warp Speed. However, according to critics, his response to the crisis was at times both misleading and damaging, ranging from an assurance that "we have it totally under control. It's one person coming in from China. It's going to be just fine" to claiming "I think we are in a good place" the day after the U.S. death toll hit 130,000.

Two days before the election on 3 November, the number of Americans killed by the virus passed 230,000 as the nation grappled with the second-worst death rate per capita on the planet. On top of this, federal debt skyrocketed (admittedly fuelled in large part by the relief fund required to keep America going).

Overall, Trump's response to the pandemic did not seem to effect his prospects in the election. The successes and failures of his presidency prior to the outbreak had only served to harden the beliefs of his supporters and critics, with both camps equally passionate about their differing views of his time in office. Fittingly for such a bombastic, outspoken and proud man, Trump's reign would not end quietly.

CHAPTER FIVE

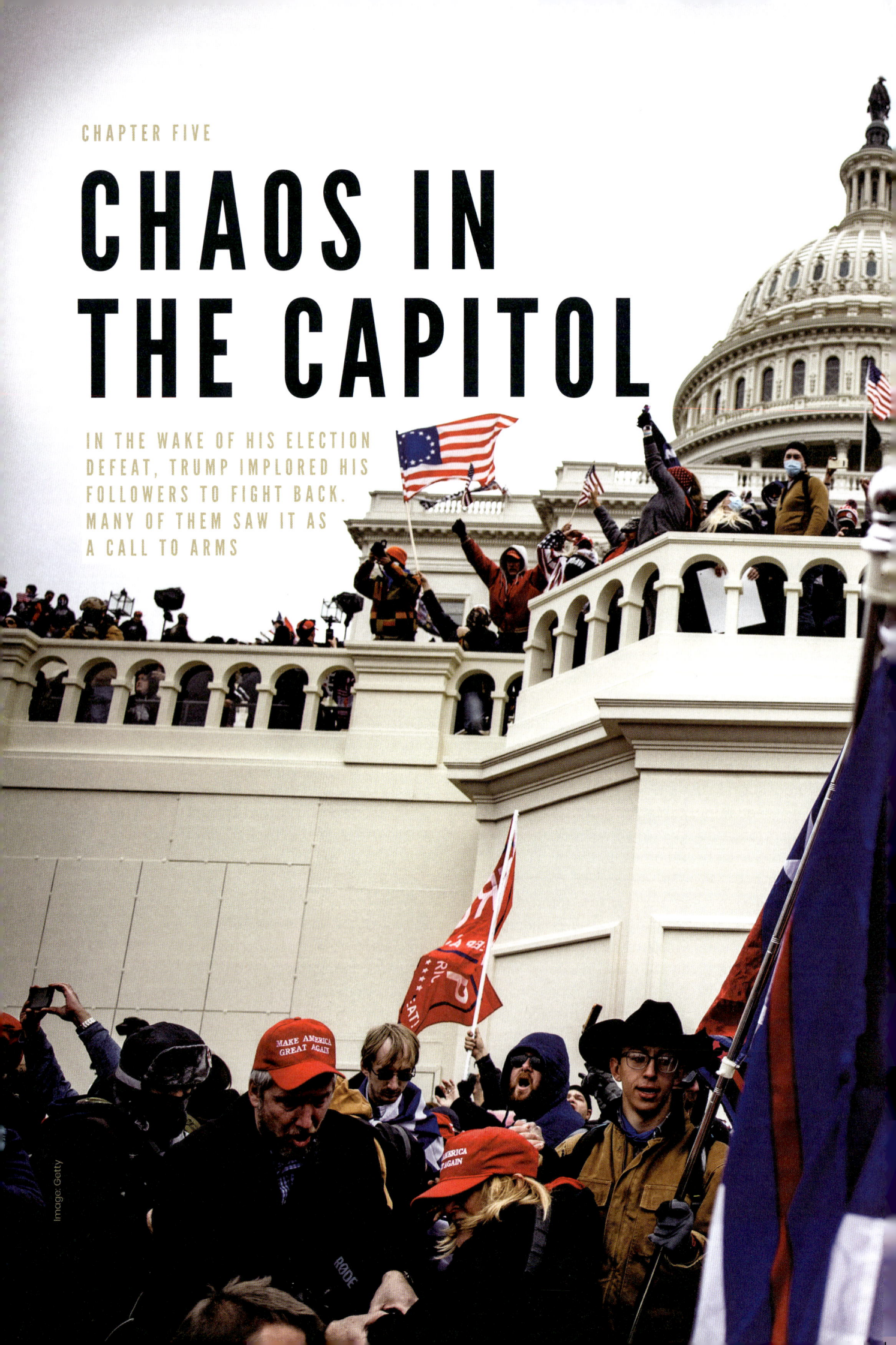

CHAOS IN THE CAPITOL

IN THE WAKE OF HIS ELECTION DEFEAT, TRUMP IMPLORED HIS FOLLOWERS TO FIGHT BACK. MANY OF THEM SAW IT AS A CALL TO ARMS

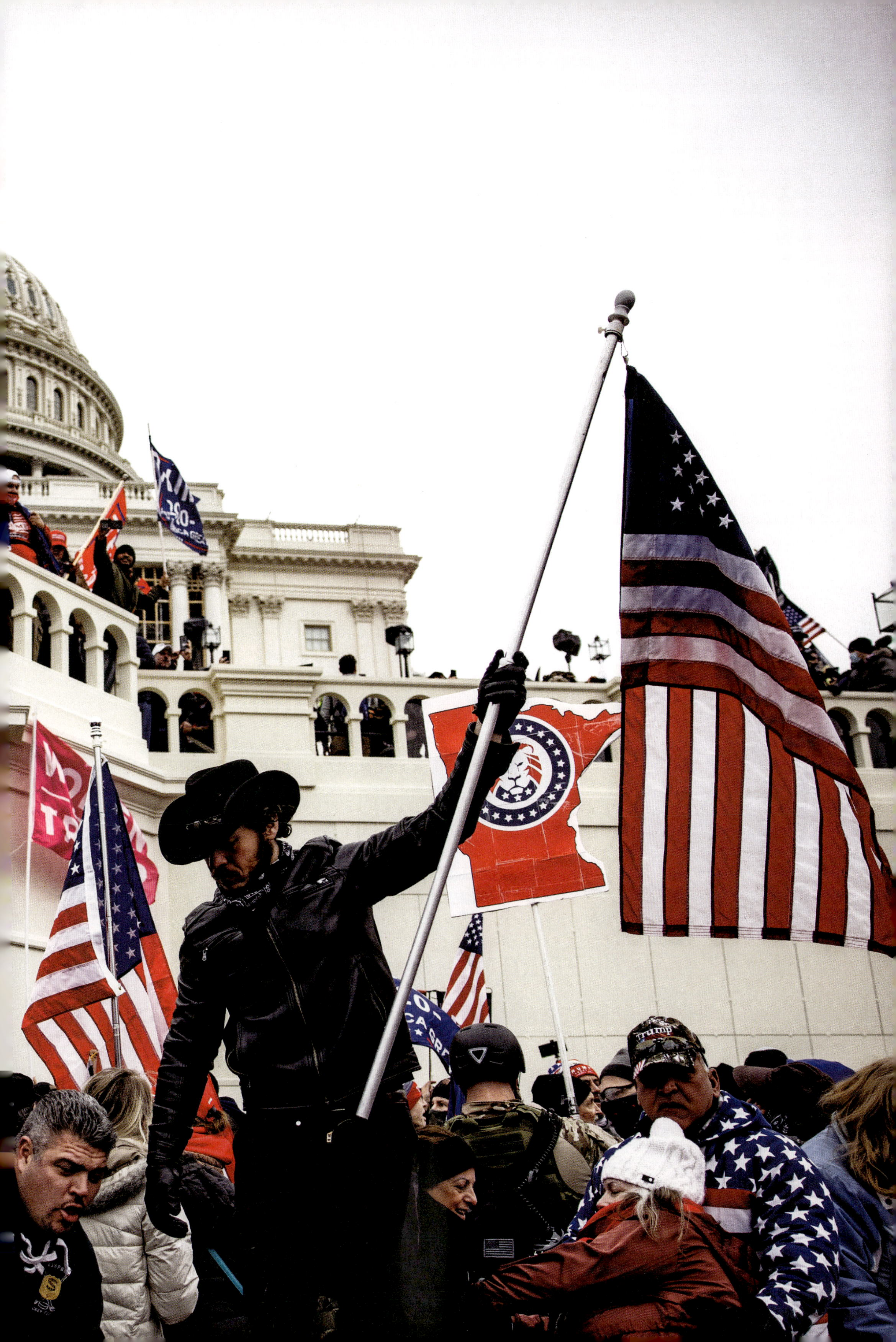
Trump

• CHAPTER FIVE •

The 2020 United States presidential election was one of the most contentious and controversial in American history, held against the backdrop of a global pandemic that affected everything from campaigning to how citizens were allowed to vote. In the wake of Trump's victory in 2016, Republicans and Democrats had become ever more ideologically opposed, with much disagreement over how the Trump administration had reacted to Covid-19 itself and the virus' negative impact on the economy, as well as issues such as racial justice, healthcare and immigration. The deep-seated tension between the two leading parties led to the highest voter turnout in 120 years, with over 158 million votes being cast nationwide.

With concerns about safe social distancing at polling stations amid the spread of the virus, there was a surge in mail-in and early voting, especially among Democrats, who were generally more fearful of the pandemic. While these atypical measures were implemented to ensure public safety, they also sowed scepticism and allegations of voter fraud, which were popularised on social media platforms for months ahead of election day on 3 November. In the run-up to the polls President Trump had repeatedly publicised his frustrations over these procedures, fearing they would weaken the integrity of the election and frequently suggesting that the result would be rigged against him if mail-in voting became widespread.

While the president's claims were refuted by multiple sources, his worries quickly spread among his followers, who supported and shared his views. With Republican politicians and voters alike spreading this narrative in a bid to uncover the truth and uphold democracy, several protests against the increase in mail-in voting were held, with many of Trump's supporters refusing to use mail-in ballots altogether so that their vote couldn't be destroyed, lost or otherwise meddled with. But from the other side, theories began to emerge that Trump was purposefully hindering the United States Postal Service (USPS) to interfere with postal voting amid the 2020 USPS crisis.

In July, the newly appointed postmaster general, Louis DeJoy, implemented cost-cutting measures

Brad Raffensperger addresses the press in regards to delayed ballot counting in Georgia

• CHAOS IN THE CAPITOL •

Some supporters covered their faces while participating in the protests in order to remain anonymous

Thousands of Trump supporters crowded into Washington, D.C., on 6 January 2021

Police officers attended the Capitol in full riot gear

• CHAPTER FIVE •

'Stop the Steal' became a slogan that carried as much weight as 'Make America Great Again'

Some attendees wore costumes, and many more carried pro-Trump signs and flags

and operational changes including reductions in overtime, removal of mail-sorting machines and reduced hours at post offices, all of which resulted in the slowing down of the delivery of mail. As DeJoy was a Trump-appointed official, the president's critics voiced concerns that this was an attempt to delay postal votes so much that many wouldn't arrive in time and would therefore remain uncounted. Trump also opposed the House of Representatives in providing more funding for USPS, which was again construed by some as him attempting to block postal votes.

Ultimately, the changes DeJoy wanted to make were postponed until after November due to public outcry and congressional scrutiny, and the vast majority of mail-in ballots were delivered in a timely manner.

With concerns over the legitimacy of postal voting continuing to spread, mirroring Trump's repeated assertions that mail-in ballots were susceptible to tampering, forgery and theft, other methods were employed to try and reduce their impact. In Pennsylvania, a key swing state, lawsuits were filed in an attempt to stop the use of ballot drop boxes if they weren't located at an election office, limiting where ballots could be taken. There were also calls for mail-in ballots to be discounted if they weren't properly enclosed inside a secrecy sleeve. As election day grew closer, allegations of deceased individuals voting, undocumented immigrants casting ballots and voting machines being manipulated to switch votes to Biden began circulating, further casting doubt on what many saw as the most high-stakes election in years.

"LAWSUITS WERE FILED IN AN ATTEMPT TO STOP THE USE OF BALLOT DROP BOXES"

A protestor carries the lectern used by House Speaker Nancy Pelosi through the Capitol

Image: Getty

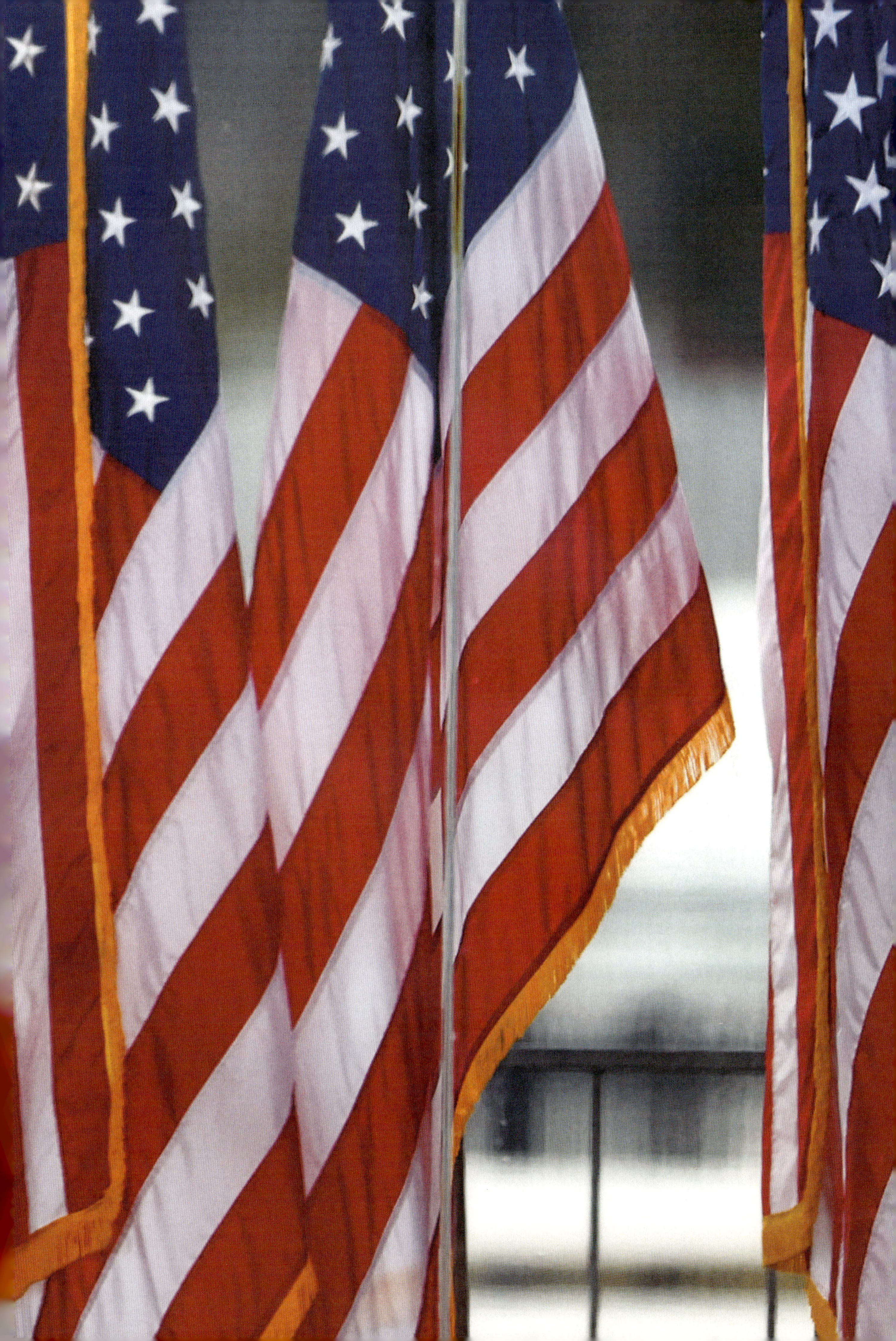

• CHAPTER FIVE •

Due to over 43 per cent of voters submitting their ballots by mail there were extensive delays to vote counts in certain states, especially in those that were almost too close to call. Counts were monitored closely by federal, state and local authorities, as well as independent organisations and observers who were concerned about voter fraud. With the votes from sparsely populated rural states giving the incumbent president an early lead, Trump soon claimed premature victories in Pennsylvania, North Carolina and Georgia, despite counting still being underway. In Georgia, an extremely narrow margin triggered a recount, further delaying the election result. As Trump began to see his lead crumble as large cities like Minneapolis, New York and Portland announced their results, his claims of fraud resurfaced, calling for reexamination in those areas.

Democrat demonstrators argued against Trump's challenges to these results, believing them to be unfounded. Outside of voting centres in Phoenix, Detroit and Philadelphia that were still counting ballots – increasingly in favour of Biden – Trump supporters urged the counts to be stopped in fear that 'Sleepy Joe' could still claim victory in

Tweets from the former president were used to try and show he supported the Capitol riot

pivotal states. Meanwhile, in places where Biden's lead was shrinking they called for every vote to be counted, the irony of which was not lost. In an attempt to stop the count in certain states, lawsuits were filed that suggested Republican observers were not allowed access to ballot counting or that late votes were being counted. However, as there was a lack of evidence these cases were dismissed.

In a massive upset for Republicans across the nation, Biden was declared the winner of the

The Capitol suffered millions of dollars' worth of damage during the protests

• CHAOS IN THE CAPITOL •

Jake Angeli, the 'QAnon Shaman', became one of the most iconic faces of the Capitol riot

• 85 •

Trump proudly holds a newspaper announcing his acquittal

Fox headquarters displays updates on the second impeachment trial

election with 306 electoral votes to Trump's 232 – the same divide that had given Trump the win in 2016. Despite the results, Trump refused to accept that he had lost, reviving his earlier claims and urging officials in close-call states to "find the votes" that he needed to win the election and begin his second term. With Trump's refusal to concede, cracks began to show in the Republican Party, with a few officials and others close to Trump advising him to accept defeat with grace rather than pursue further legal action. But Trump's pride was wounded, and his administration went ahead with attempting to overturn what many across the country believed to be a fraudulent result.

Officials appealed to the Georgia Supreme Court to negate Biden's win in the crucial state. Trump's personal attorney Rudy Giuliani also petitioned the Supreme Court to rescind the results from Pennsylvania, while 126 Republicans of the House of Representatives appealed to have Biden's wins in Michigan, Pennsylvania, Wisconsin and Georgia repealed. While legal challenges and disputes surrounding the election were widespread, the vast majority of cases were dismissed by both state and federal courts for lack of evidence or standing. At the request of the former president and in accordance with Georgia law, a third tally of the state's votes was made between 11 and 18 November. Concerns were raised about a small discrepancy between the totals, which dropped Biden's lead slightly, but not enough to change the outcome.

Photos taken on 6 January were shown during hearings by a select committee

"TRUMP RALLIED HIS SUPPORTERS TO WIN BACK THE ELECTION THAT HE ALLEGED HAD BEEN STOLEN"

Yet Trump refused to back down. He used his platform on social media and public appearances to continue to dispute the legitimacy of the results, rallying his supporters to challenge the certification of the Electoral College and win back the election that he alleged had been stolen from him – hence the slogan 'Stop the Steal' gaining popularity. Supporters of this movement organised protests, rallies and social media campaigns to demand investigations into voter fraud, while policymakers continued to pursue various lawsuits and come up with other ways Trump could stay in power. One of the most extreme ideas came from former national security advisor Michael Flynn, who suggested martial law be declared so the election could be re-run under military supervision.

By the turn of 2021, multiple recounts, audits and court rulings had found no evidence of fraud that could have affected the outcome of the election, and plans had been going ahead to ready Biden for the presidency. Critics of the 'Stop the Steal' movement argued it was no more than a disinformation campaign aimed at undermining confidence in the democratic process. However, many Trump supporters saw their refusal to accept their loss as a form of political activism and civic duty rather than an attempt to subvert democracy. It was this duty that brought tens of thousands of supporters to Washington, D.C., on 6 January – the same day former vice president Mike Pence was to oversee a congressional session in the Capitol to count electoral votes and finalise Biden's win.

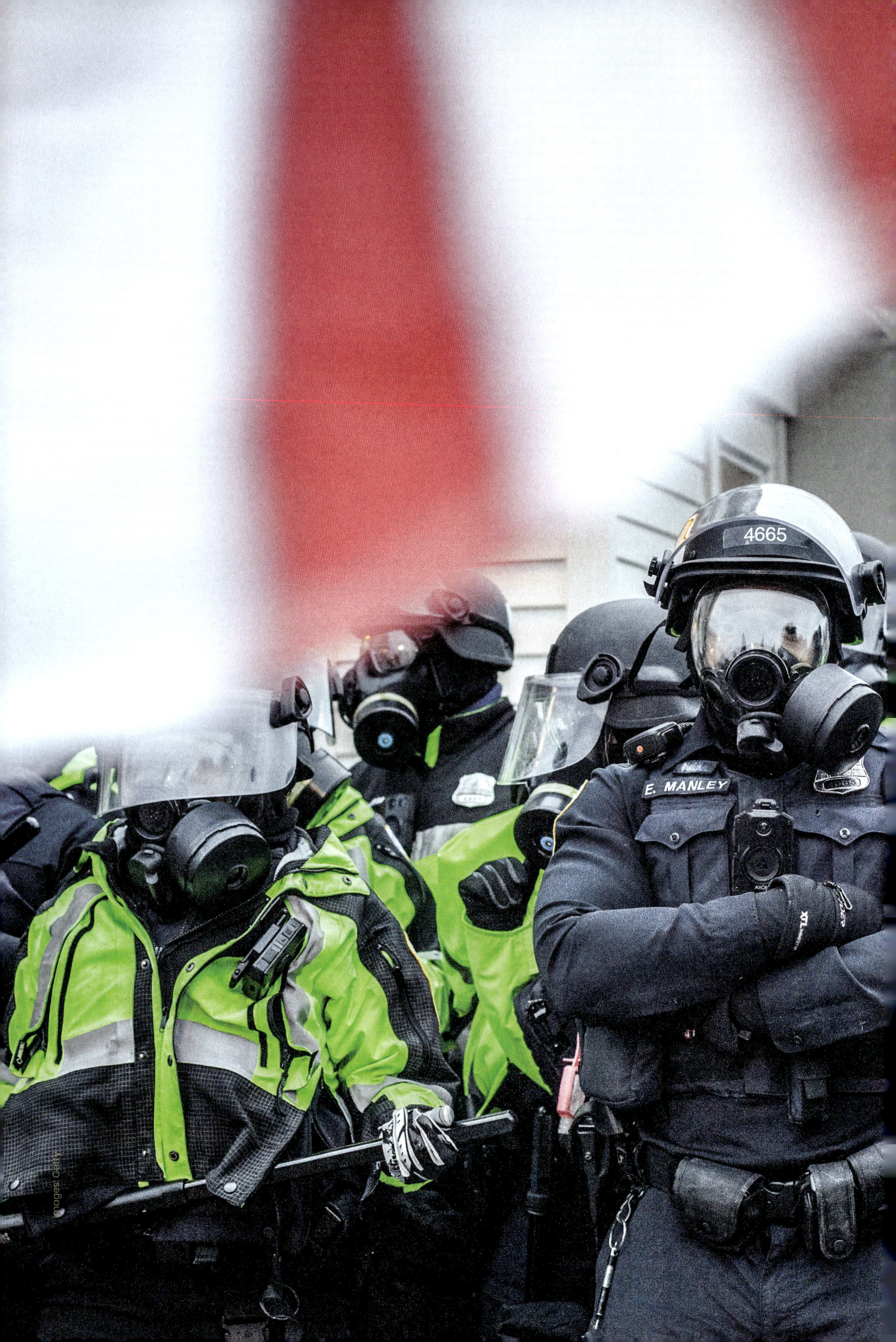

Images: Getty

6 JAN 12:16 P.M. TRUMP TELLS THE CROWD:
"I KNOW THAT EVERYONE HERE WILL SOON BE MARCHING OVER TO THE CAPITOL BUILDING TO PEACEFULLY AND PATRIOTICALLY MAKE YOUR VOICES HEARD"

FINISHING HIS SPEECH WITH:
"WE FIGHT. WE FIGHT LIKE HELL, AND IF YOU DON'T FIGHT LIKE HELL, YOU'RE NOT GOING TO HAVE A COUNTRY ANY MORE"

• CHAPTER FIVE •

In an impassioned speech at the Ellipse, Trump decried the election to thousands of flag-waving followers and urged Pence to block Congress' declaration of the win. He implored the eager crowd to march on the Capitol and make their voices heard, to "fight like hell" and stop the government officials inside from certifying the election. His most fanatical supporters – including members of right-wing groups – took his words as a direct order, shouting cries of "storm the Capitol" and "fight for Trump" as they headed for the landmark. Waves of protestors pushed through barricades and displaced the Capitol Police, with some resorting to violence. Everything devolved into chaos as the building was breached, with the ever-increasing mob smashing windows and scaling walls to make their way inside.

The insurrection continued for several hours, with the police overwhelmed by hordes of rioters who vandalised offices, ransacked the building and brandished flags and firearms. Many of the trespassers posed for photos and broadcast footage from inside the Capitol to their social media, evidently proud of their actions. The convened officials – including Pence – were evacuated for their safety, successfully delaying the certification of the Electoral College results. After hours of disorder, police reinforcements managed to bring the Capitol back under control, though by this point the riot had resulted in injuries to over 140 police officers and many more attendees, the deaths of five individuals and millions in damage to the Capitol Building.

Though hardly any arrests were made directly following the attack on the Capitol, the extensive footage circulating online was later used to identify many who had taken part, people who were later charged and convicted for various crimes. The former president himself also came under fire despite not actively being involved, accused of inciting violence with his speech,

Supporters from both sides attended vote counts in Philadelphia

ignoring multiple pleas for assistance and failing to promptly instruct his supporters to leave peacefully. As a result, on 13 January Trump was impeached with a vote of 232 to 197. Ten of these votes came from Republican members of the House of Representatives, making it bipartisan. Trump would now go down in history as the first president to be impeached twice.

While awaiting his trial in the Senate, Trump neglected to attend Biden's inauguration on 20 January, breaking a long-standing tradition. Many saw this as a continuation of his refusal to acknowledge the legitimacy of the election, something he would again argue during his trial.

After five days of evidence being presented and discussed, Trump was acquitted on 13 February with a vote of 57 to 43. While a majority voted to convict, they fell short of the two-thirds needed for conviction under the Constitution, thus Trump was acquitted, avoiding a costly conviction or being banned from serving in office in the future.

His acquittal renewed his reputation in the eyes of many voters, and today a large number of Republicans still trust in Trump's claims that the 2020 election was taken from them. Many are ready to do all they can to protect the integrity of 2024's rematch.

"AFTER HOURS OF DISORDER, POLICE MANAGED TO BRING THE CAPITOL BACK UNDER CONTROL"

Security around the Capitol was tightened on 4 March 2021 due to a perceived threat from QAnon to attack the building

CHAPTER SIX

THESE DISUNITED STATES

AS WHAT IS LIKELY TO BE THE NASTIEST ELECTION IN LIVING MEMORY LOOMS, THE U.S. HAS RARELY BEEN SO ANGRY AND DIVIDED. THE COMING RACE FOR THE WHITE HOUSE IS SHAPING UP TO BE A BATTLE FOR THE VERY SOUL OF AMERICA

Image: Getty

• CHAPTER SIX •

It's being hailed as the nastiest presidential campaign in U.S. history, a contest in which 81-year-old Joe Biden and 77-year-old Donald Trump will lock horns once again for the right to hold the most powerful position in the Western world against a backdrop of scandal, lawsuits and increasingly personal verbal attacks.

In many ways this fractious build-up to the impending U.S. presidential election on 5 November 2024 reflects increasing political polarisation in America over the last decade.

According to a piece in the *Washington Post* in January 2024, political differences now stem more from a visceral dislike of the opposition rather than disagreements over each other's policies.

"It's feelings based," says Lilliana Mason, a political scientist at Johns Hopkins University and author of *Uncivil Agreement: How Politics Became Our Identity*. "It's polarisation that's based on our feelings for each other, not based on extremely divergent policy preferences."

There's plenty of research to back this up. Raw emotion rather than rational thought is what's driving many people's voting habits. This is a whole new political landscape. Whatever transpires between now and the election, the result will leave a lasting impact on American politics for years and decades to come.

As President Biden embarks on what promises to be a long, hard slog over the coming months, he holds one important asset that he didn't have the first time around – four years hands-on experience in the top job.

From the outset, tackling climate change was integral to Biden's plans. One of his first objectives following his inauguration on 20 January 2021 was to bring the U.S. back within the Paris Agreement. He set out to implement a shift towards energy transition, weaning the country off fossil fuels and beginning the process of reversing rising global temperatures. He revoked a Keystone XL pipeline permit and suspended the leasing of oil and gas on public lands. He also announced the creation of a so-called 'Build Back Better' plan, which would entail heavy investment in environmental initiatives, including investments in technology to reduce America's greenhouse gas emissions.

A piece assessing Biden's first term in office published in *The Washington Post* on 22 October

Desparate Afghans race towards an airport in Kabul hoping to board a flight out of the country following the chaotic U.S. withdrawal

Trump has vowed to end the war in Ukraine "in one day"

"POLITICAL DIFFERENCES NOW STEM FROM VISCERAL DISLIKE OF THE OPPOSITION"

THESE DISUNITED STATES

• CHAPTER SIX •

Having run on the promise of reuniting America, Biden's
Philadelphia speech achieved the opposite

2022 and written by Ashley Parker, Tyler Pager and Michael Scherer, acknowledged Biden's achievements: "With the narrowest control of Congress in decades, he passed laws on Covid relief, infrastructure, climate change, manufacturing, gun regulation and prescription drug prices that in most cases had spent years on Democratic wish lists"

However, the piece also acknowledged Biden's shortcomings, noting that some people closest to the president described an administration achieving significant victories while repeatedly running up against "the limits of the federal bureaucracy, a tissue-thin majority in Congress and a deeply divided nation".

It also noted that while Biden was elected on the promise of competent governance, he quickly learned that "the most rigorous science and best expert advice could not protect the country from new waves of disease and economic hardship."

As is often the case with U.S. presidents, the best-laid plans can be thwarted by external events. For Biden, such an outcome occurred on 22 February 2022 when Russia invaded Ukraine. It was the largest attack on a European country since World War II and almost overnight the prices for oil and natural gas skyrocketed.

As journalist Oliver Milman noted in *The Guardian* in September 2022: "The Russian tanks and armoured vehicles had barely begun to roll into Ukraine before the fossil fuel industry in the U.S. had swung into action. A letter was swiftly dispatched to the White House urging an immediate escalation in gas production and exports to Europe ahead of an anticipated energy crunch."

The letter allegedly demanded "more drilling on U.S. public lands; the swift approval of proposed gas export terminals; and pressure on the Federal Energy Regulatory Commission, an independent agency, to greenlight pending gas pipelines".

From left to right: Chris Christie, Nikki Haley, Ron DeSantis and Vivek Ramaswamy all failed in their bids to beat Trump to the Republican nomination

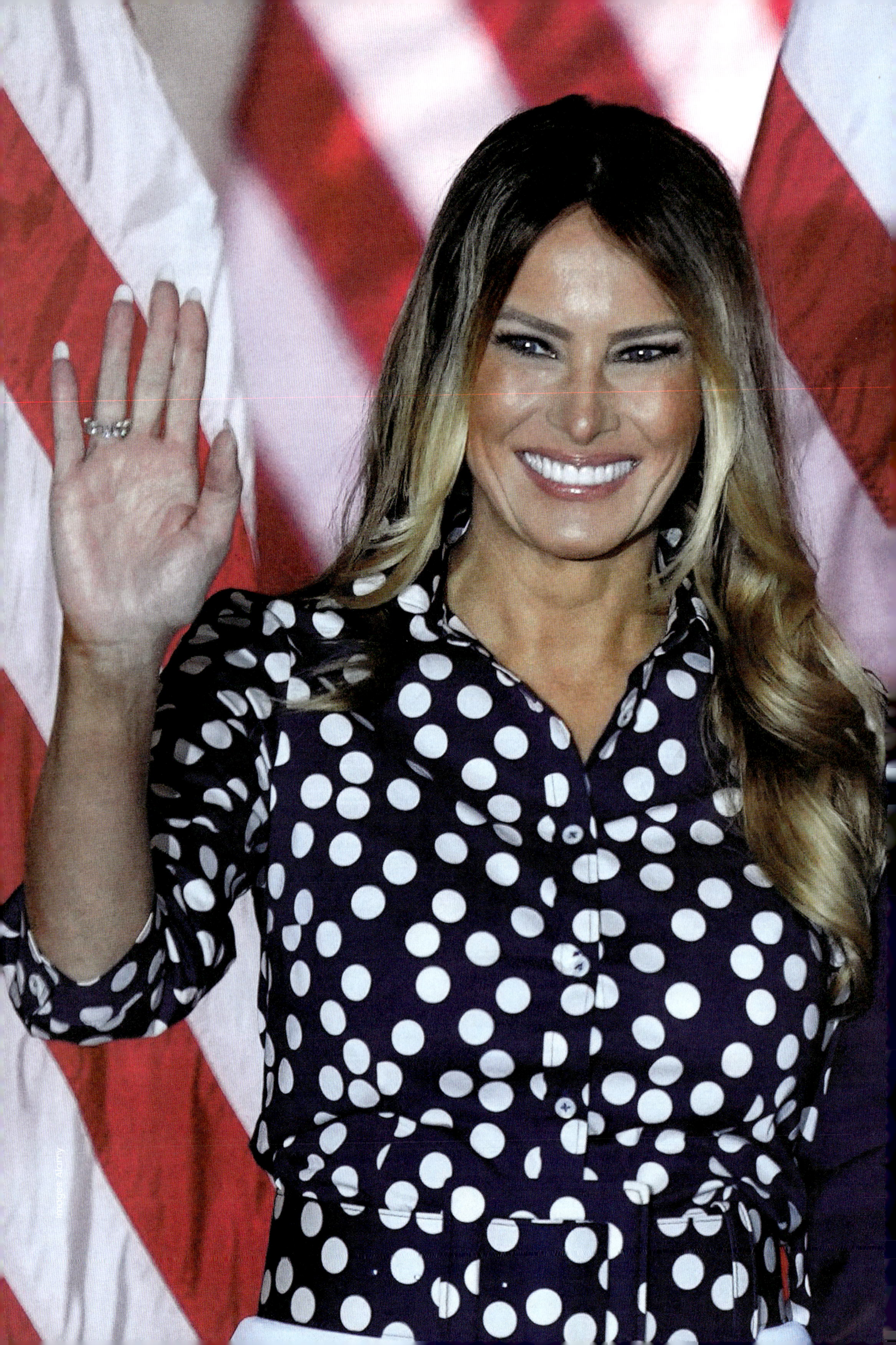

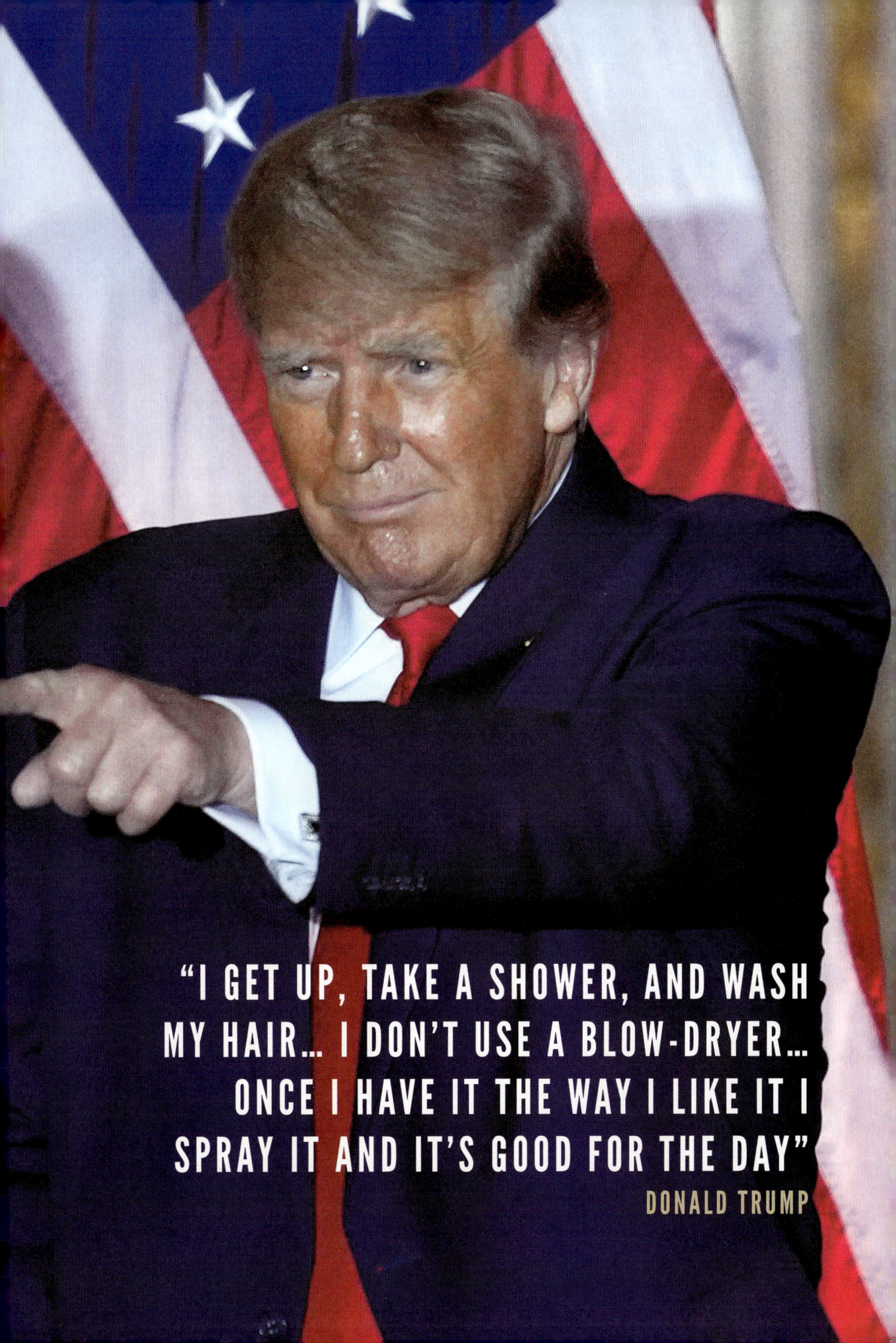

> "I GET UP, TAKE A SHOWER, AND WASH MY HAIR... I DON'T USE A BLOW-DRYER... ONCE I HAVE IT THE WAY I LIKE IT I SPRAY IT AND IT'S GOOD FOR THE DAY"
>
> DONALD TRUMP

CHAPTER SIX

This spelt disaster for Biden's commitment to wind down fossil fuel production. Within weeks, he and his administration had been compelled to accept the gas industry's major demands as policy. It wasn't the first crisis he'd had to grapple with either.

When Biden took office the Covid-19 pandemic was still running rife. He wasted no time attacking the anti-vaccine movement and pushed for 100 million U.S. workers to receive jabs. He also presided over a broad distribution of vaccines and a $1.9-trillion economic relief package. Like other world leaders, he was keen to kick-start the economy, but he was criticised for being too quick in declaring the pandemic over. After the increased roll-out of vaccines the deaths slowed, but 1.1 million Americans still ultimately died.

When it comes to issues concerning American voters, the economy is right up there. Recent research by Reuters shows that Americans now view the economy as the biggest problem facing their country.

Biden ran on a promise to reinvigorate the U.S. economy by taxing the wealthy and large companies more, and under his administration job growth reached levels not seen since the 1960s. However, inflation also hit a 40-year high in July 2022, fuelled partly by pandemic spending and problems in supply chains that led to gasoline costing over $5 a gallon by the summer of 2022. Some of the blame was placed at Biden's feet due to his increased spending, and as of February 2023 his policies have added an astonishing $6 trillion to America's national debt, which currently stands at over $34 trillion and growing, making him by far the biggest-spending president in U.S. history. On top of this, businesses and consumers have, according to the Bureau of Labor Statistics, seen an 18 per cent rise in the prices they pay for goods.

Biden has also overseen the worst border crisis in American history as illegal immigrants stream over the Mexican border by the thousands, a situation greatly exacerbated by the decision to strip away

Trump has promised to deal robustly with China and Iran, nations viewed as hostile to the U.S.

THESE DISUNITED STATES

Trump will hope that the passion of his fans is reflected in the voting booth

Ever the savvy businessman, Trump's phrase has inspired a wealth of merchandise

Trump has called on America's NATO allies to spend more on their defence budgets

border security measures (since Biden took office over 7.2 million illegal immigrants have entered the U.S. via the southern border). When the governor of Texas, Greg Abbott, vowed to ignore a U.S. Supreme Court order to tear down razor wire erected on the Texan border, Biden found himself embroiled in a divisive row as governors across the States backed Abbott and offered to send troops to help patrol the border.

Further afield, while the wars in Ukraine and the Middle East cannot of course be attributed to Biden, it is worth noting that both regions were extremely calm during Trump's presidency. However, both were apportioned blame in a State Department report on the U.S. withdrawal from Afghanistan that was published in the summer of 2023. "The decisions of both President Trump and President Biden to end the U.S. military mission posed significant challenges for the [State] Department as it sought to maintain a robust diplomatic and assistance presence in Kabul and provide continued support to the Afghan government and people," the report stated.

As Biden and Trump gear up for the gruelling months of campaigning leading up to the November election, all the signs are that this will be an embittered and deeply personal contest, especially if Biden's controversial speech in Philadelphia a few years back is anything to go by. Standing before Independence Hall in September 2022, flanked by soldiers and bathed in deep red lighting, Biden railed against Trump and his followers: "MAGA Republicans do not respect the Constitution. They do not believe in the rule of law." Accusing them of holding "a dagger to the throat of our democracy," he implied MAGA supporters were a "cancer" and said they "spread fear and lies – lies told for profit and power".

Given that such distinct battle lines have already been drawn, it's no surprise *The Telegraph* recently predicted it would be "the nastiest presidential campaign in U.S. history." It's a battle Trump was always destined to fight.

In reality, the Republican Party has only ever had one clear candidate: Trump. In 2023, there was a crowded field of candidates, namely Florida governor Ron DeSantis, former ambassador to

> "BIDEN IMPLIED MAGA SUPPORTERS WERE A 'CANCER' AND SAID THEY 'SPREAD FEAR AND LIES – LIES TOLD FOR PROFIT AND POWER'"

the United Nations and former governor of South Carolina, Nikki Haley, and wealth management executive Vivek Ramaswamy.

DeSantis initially polled in a close second behind Trump, but his numbers declined through 2023. Ramaswamy's polling numbers experienced a surge in mid-2023 but then dropped. By contrast, Haley's campaign really began to gather momentum in the final months of 2023, although even she didn't come close to Trump, who enjoyed a consistent lead in the polls.

In the 15 January Iowa caucuses Trump landed a decisive victory, with DeSantis narrowly beating Haley, while Ramaswamy came in fourth place. DeSantis and Ramaswamy then dropped out of the race, leaving Trump and Haley as the only Republican candidates.

At the 23 January New Hampshire primary Trump defeated Haley, although the margin was smaller than it had been at the Iowa caucuses. One month later, in the 24 February South Carolina primary, Haley was defeated by Trump again. But on 3 March, Haley beat Trump to win the District of Columbia primary in Washington, D.C, thereby becoming the first woman in American history to win a Republican primary or caucus. Two days later, on 5 March, she bested Trump again, securing an additional win in the Vermont primary,

★★★★★
TEXT TRUMP TO 88022
STOP BIDEN'S
BORDER
BLOODBATH
GRAND RAPIDS, MICHIGAN
2024

Image: Alamy

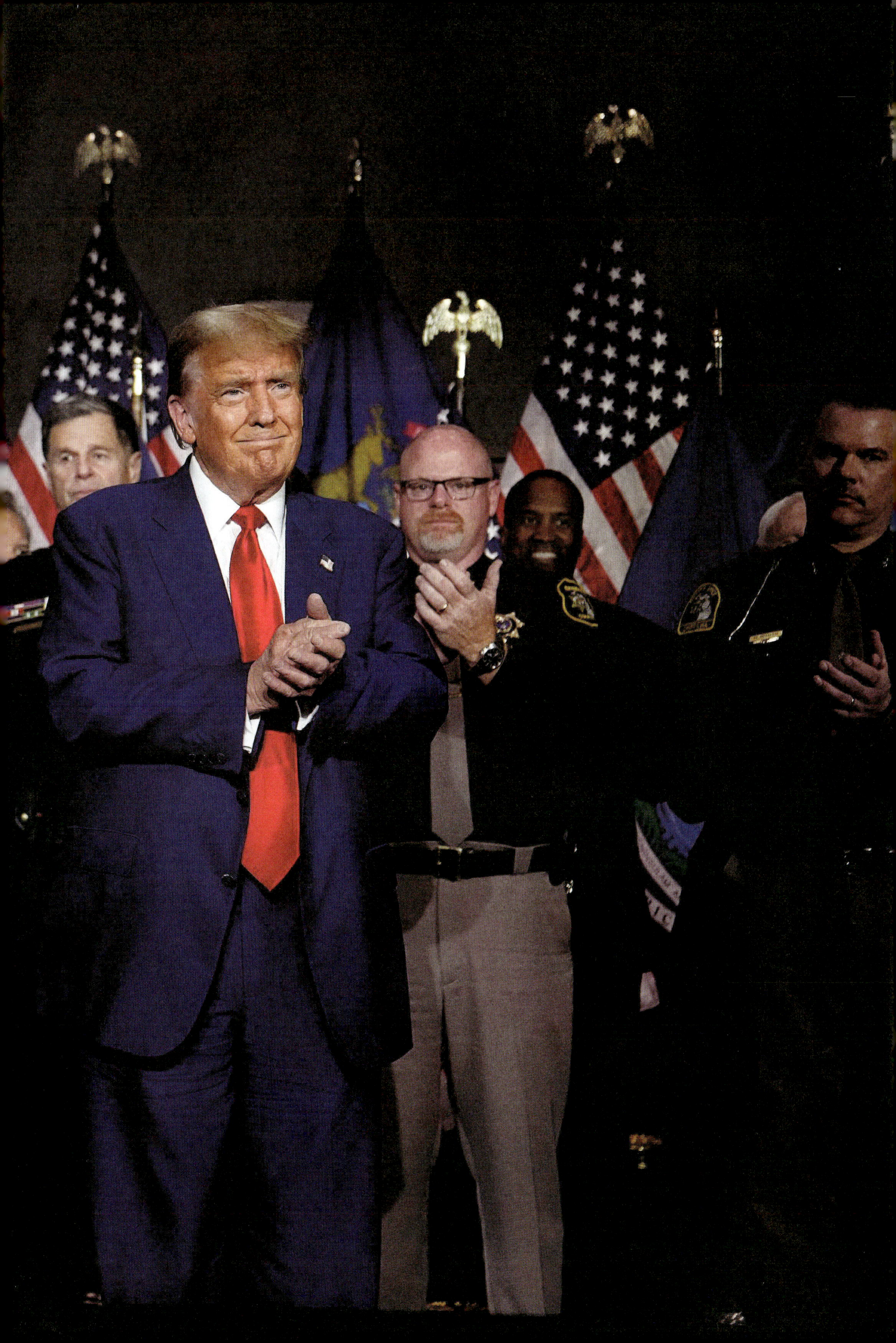

CHAPTER SIX

her biggest victory since the start of the GOP primary season.

Despite these successes, Trump was way ahead. Haley was soundly defeated in the coast-to-coast Super Tuesday contest and reluctantly withdrew from the campaign on 6 March 2024.

"The time has now come to suspend my campaign," said Haley, announcing her decision during a three-minute speech in Charleston, South Carolina. "It is now up to Donald Trump to earn the votes of those in our party and beyond who did not support him, and I hope he does that."

Haley, who had been Trump's UN ambassador, became the first prominent woman of colour to seek the Republican nomination for U.S. president. Unlike nearly all Trump's other Republican rivals, Haley noticeably failed to endorse him. By contrast, she challenged Trump to earn the support of her voters, and said it was his "time for choosing".

In the final weeks of her campaign, Haley had become the leader of the Republican Party's disparate anti-Trump movement. Although initially reluctant to take on her former boss, Haley embarked on a series of increasingly direct and personal attacks on Trump, questioning his mental fitness and his loyalty to the U.S. Constitution.

Haley had been determined to remain in the race until at least Super Tuesday, but in the wake of disappointing results she admitted she had no viable route forward. "I said I wanted Americans to have their voices heard. I have done that," she said on 6 March. "I have no regrets."

Before her speech, Trump had attacked Haley on social media, downplaying her win in Vermont and accusing her of drawing support from "Radical Left Democrats". But Haley has always appealed to a key demographic, as *The Guardian* reported on the day that she dropped out of the race. "Despite enduring a long string of losses, exit polls showed her strength among suburban women and independents – key constituencies in a general election that she warned Trump was continuing to alienate. A sizable share of her supporters – and Republican voters more broadly – say they would not vote for a candidate convicted of a crime."

Trump's now infamous police mugshot

And therein lies a problem for Trump. Eight years on from being sworn in as president, he is mired in lawsuits that some marginal voters will be unable to ignore. Trump is the subject of four criminal cases and several civil suits.

On 25 March 2024, he appeared at a press conference in New York in connection with his criminal trial on 34 charges concerning hush-money payments to an adult film star and a civil fraud case in which he must post a $175-million bond while appealing a $454-million judgement.

Trump also faces 14 criminal charges related to election subversion and 40 arising from his retention of classified information.

As the *Financial Times* pointed out on 24 February 2024: "That means the presumptive Republican nominee will be spending a lot of time in courtrooms ahead of voting day in November."

On 17 February 2024, the *FT*'s New York-based legal correspondent Joe Miller outlined the potential impact of ongoing legal cases. "Financially and politically they will pile pressure on the former president as he gears up for a

"TRUMP WILL BE SPENDING A LOT OF TIME IN COURTROOMS AHEAD OF VOTING DAY"

Trump salutes his supporters after a press conference following a hearing in his hush money criminal case

Trump's former lawyer Alina Habba condemns the verdict that saw author E. Jean Carroll awarded $83 million after winning her defamation case against the former president

• CHAPTER SIX •

fiercely fought and expensive general election. They also demonstrate the limits of Trump's go-to legal strategy of attempting to delay proceedings by any means possible, including the lodging of appeals at every stage and the playing of various pending cases off each other, to complicate the scheduling of any potential trials."

But despite the legal proceedings, the colossal financial outlay and the pressure to hit the campaign trail with all the vim and vigour he can muster, Trump has seemingly performed well in the polls despite having minimal campaign events on his agenda.

While Biden barnstormed swing states across the nation, Trump was barely seen in public, spending much of his time in southern Florida, fundraising, orchestrating his campaign and playing golf. Wooing potential donors to the campaign has been his primary focus.

So far, Trump has unveiled a number of policies for a second term, as CNN detailed on 6 March.

These include reversing Joe Biden's commitment to electric vehicles; axing programmes that promote gender transition; closing the Department of Education to send "all education and education work and needs back to the states"; waging war on drug cartels and asking Congress to ensure that drug smugglers and human traffickers can receive the death penalty for their "heinous acts"; appointing a special prosecutor to investigate Joe Biden and his family; and replacing the Affordable Care Act, known as Obamacare. "Getting much better Healthcare than Obamacare for the American people will be a priority of the Trump Administration," he wrote on Truth Social.

Trump's policies also include implementing an 'America first' trade agenda that would impose the same tariffs that other countries impose on the U.S. "It's called you screw us and we screw you," he told a rally in South Carolina.

Not surprisingly, Biden and Trump are both publicly oozing confidence while at every given

Trump and Governor Abbott pass the razor wire placed along the Texan border that the Supreme Court demanded be cut

Around 52 per cent of Trump supporters identify as 'very conservative', and his popularity with female voters is on the rise

opportunity shooting broadsides at each other in what, as commentators predicted, is becoming an increasingly vicious campaign. On 25 March, a Biden campaign spokesperson described Trump as "weak and desperate – both as a man and a candidate," adding that "his campaign can't raise money, he is uninterested in campaigning outside his country club, and every time he opens his mouth, he pushes moderate and suburban voters away with his dangerous agenda."

Trump's team, meanwhile, honed in on Biden's campaign endeavours. Trump spokesperson Karoline Leavitt said Biden "looks like a lost puppy any time he ventures onto the campaign trail," before going on to accuse Biden's campaign of limiting his events to "stops at field offices with a few paid staffers who look less enthused than attendees at a funeral". Leavitt went on to add that "Joe Biden's campaign is a failing, boring, disaster. President Trump is building the greatest political movement in history."

Despite having no visible campaign presence by the end of March 2024, Trump was ahead in Arizona, Georgia, Nevada and North Carolina. But Biden and Trump were tied in Pennsylvania, where Trump had a six-point lead in February. The two candidates were also tied in Michigan. But according to Bloomberg News and Morning Consult, Biden was ahead of Trump by a point in Wisconsin. This led to one Democratic strategist proclaiming that "the Biden bump is real," suggesting that Biden was gaining on Trump in six battleground states.

But as ever, different media outlets have different findings, making it tricky to accurately gauge the overall picture. A report in *The Telegraph* on 27 March 2024 concluded that it was Trump who had a narrow lead over Biden, proclaiming Trump to be the clear frontrunner.

In March, Trump campaign spokesperson Jason Miller pointed to Trump's 47-43 per cent lead across the seven swing states, telling Bloomberg: "Polling continues to show that voters are sick of Joe Biden's crushing inflation, porous southern border and his insane EV mandate that will kill the U.S. auto industry."

• CHAPTER SIX •

Trump floated Truth Social on New York's Nasdaq stock exchange in March 2024. It's currently valued at over $7 billion

Trump's legal wrangles have done him little harm to date; his campaign received $4.2 million in donations in the 24 hours after his mugshot was released

The Telegraph suggested that Biden's age and the cost of living could work in Trump's favour, although it concluded that Trump must win over moderate Republicans who voted against him in the primaries. In a poll by *The Economist* referenced in *The Telegraph*, the surge in immigration across the U.S.–Mexico border was cited as one the most important election issues for many Americans.

The Telegraph reported that in an increasingly polarised United States, the fate of democracy itself has also emerged as one of the key political issues. Republicans have argued that Biden is attempting to 'weaponise' the judicial system to convict the former president.

The U.S. economy may be performing fairly well, but the day to day experience of many Americans is that they are struggling with the impact of rising inflation and the cost of living. These factors seem likely to damage Biden at the polls.

Analysts have also suggested that the president is losing the support of core Democrat voters, including young liberals, Black voters and Muslims concerned about Gaza.

In its 'U.S. Election 2024 Poll Tracker' report of 27 March 2024, *The Telegraph* suggested that Trump's poll ratings are relatively unaffected by the criminal and civil cases involving the former president. But the Telegraph does highlight the financial impact of ongoing litigation on the former president. "Mr Trump has also taken to the stand to testify in a $250-million civil fraud trial in New York, which threatens to strip him of his business empire in the city, including the iconic Trump Tower."

Trump's appearance makes him the first former president in 100 years to give evidence as a defendant in court. And as the *Telegraph* pointed out, "Exit polls from Super Tuesday also show an alarming number of Republican voters saying Mr Trump will not be fit to serve if convicted."

Much will depend on the outcome in the courtroom. The many criminal charges arranged against Trump all carry prison sentences, and he has been threatened with incarceration by Justice Juan Merchan, the judge presiding over the hush money trial, for breaching a gag order that prevents Trump from discussing people involved in the case. In a typically bullish retort, Trump shrugged off the threat: "Frankly our Constitution is much more important than jail. It's not even close. I'll do that sacrifice any day."

"TRUMP WILL WIN EVERY SWING STATE AND GET ELECTED"
STEVE EISMAN

As has often been the case with Trump, controversy could actually boost his prospects, but whether he can engage the moderate Republicans who cast their votes for Nikki Haley and galvanise support in the 'battleground' states such as Georgia, Florida, Michigan, Arizona, Pennsylvania and North Carolina remains to be seen. As of 30 April, Trump was leading in all of these states, plus Nevada and Wisconsin.

Trump himself has already written the narrative for a scenario in which he fails to win on 5 November. "If I don't get elected, it's going to be a bloodbath for the country," he said as winds whipped around an airfield in Ohio where he stood, with his red "Make America Great Again" baseball cap on, addressing supporters. "If we don't win this election, I don't think you're going to have another election."

As the campaigns gather pace over the months ahead, it seems likely that the exchanges between Trump and Biden will become ever more barbed and personal. Both men's policies and private beliefs could not be more polarised. It remains to be seen which of these two visions will be the driving force for America in the near future. If current polls are to be believed, Trump will win a very close contest.

According to Steve Eisman, an investor who made his name during the financial crash of 2008 when the American housing bubble burst, "It is completely inevitable that Donald Trump will win every single swing state and get elected." Now there's a deal that the Don would happily shake on.

Image: Getty

"THE 2024 ELECTION IS OUR LAST CHANCE TO SAVE OUR COUNTRY. THE SAME CORRUPT FORCES THAT HAVE BEEN FIGHTING US EVERY STEP OF THE WAY ARE NOW SHATTERING EVERY DEMOCRATIC NORM TO TRY TO STOP US FROM DEFEATING THEM IN THIS FINAL BATTLE"

DONALD TRUMP

THE STORY OF TRUMP

Future PLC Quay House, The Ambury, Bath, BA1 1UA

Editorial
Editor **Charles Ginger**
Senior Art Editor **Andy Downes**
Head of Art & Design **Greg Whitaker**
Editorial Director **Jon White**
Managing Director **Grainne McKenna**

Cover images
Getty

Photography
All copyrights and trademarks are recognised and respected

Advertising
Media packs are available on request
Commercial Director **Clare Dove**

International
Head of Print Licensing **Rachel Shaw**
licensing@futurenet.com
www.futurecontenthub.com

Circulation
Head of Newstrade **Tim Mathers**

Production
Head of Production **Mark Constance**
Production Project Manager **Matthew Eglinton**
Advertising Production Manager **Joanne Crosby**
Digital Editions Controller **Jason Hudson**
Production Managers **Keely Miller, Nola Cokely, Vivienne Calvert, Fran Twentyman**

Printed in the UK

Distributed by Marketforce – www.marketforce.co.uk
For enquiries, please email: mfcommunications@futurenet.com

The Story of Trump First Edition (AHB5981)
© 2024 Future Publishing Limited

We are committed to only using magazine paper which is derived from responsibly managed, certified forestry and chlorine-free manufacture. The paper in this bookazine was sourced and produced from sustainable managed forests, conforming to strict environmental and socioeconomic standards.

All contents © 2024 Future Publishing Limited or published under licence. All rights reserved. No part of this magazine may be used, stored, transmitted or reproduced in any way without the prior written permission of the publisher. Future Publishing Limited (company number 2008885) is registered in England and Wales. Registered office: Quay House, The Ambury, Bath BA1 1UA. All information contained in this publication is for information only and is, as far as we are aware, correct at the time of going to press. Future cannot accept any responsibility for errors or inaccuracies in such information. You are advised to contact manufacturers and retailers directly with regard to the price of products/services referred to in this publication. Apps and websites mentioned in this publication are not under our control. We are not responsible for their contents or any other changes or updates to them. This magazine is fully independent and not affiliated in any way with the companies mentioned herein.

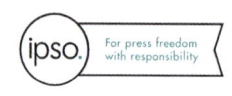

FUTURE
Connectors.
Creators.
Experience Makers.

Future plc is a public company quoted on the London Stock Exchange (symbol: FUTR)
www.futureplc.com

Chief Executive Officer **Jon Steinberg**
Non-Executive Chairman **Richard Huntingford**
Chief Financial and Strategy Officer **Penny Ladkin-Brand**

Tel +44 (0)1225 442 244

Widely Recycled

ipso For press freedom with responsibility